# Everyday Grace

## Finding your Extraordinary in Ordinary Everyday Life

Carla Marie Carlson

Norsemen Books

*For my Mom.*

With my warm wishes

Cal—

# TABLE OF CONTENTS

---

*Be strong and courageous. Do not be afraid or terrified because of them, for the Lord your God goes with you; he will never leave you nor forsake you.*

*Deuteronomy 31:6*

## PREPARING FOR CHANGE

"Take a quarter" they said. "Keep your shoes on and run to the payphone across the street if you need help." That was the extent of my safety training. I was 21 years old and I was starting my first in-home care placement with a family identified as high risk for violence and abuse. It was a legitimate social work position and also my first real job. My resume to date consisted only of several food service gigs so this job was a giant leap up the employment ladder. I was excited. I was going to live with this family and I was going to make a difference.

Raised in an upper-middle class family, I had a fairly routine and uneventful childhood. My parents both professionals, I grew up learning to "do my part" in order to ensure that everything ran smooth. There was little conflict, most of it related to whose turn it was to load the dishwasher. I do remember seeing my Mom once slide the kitchen door closed after a fight with my Dad. I was pretty sure they had been arguing and she was crying. For a moment I felt sad for her, but then I promptly left to play with friends and forgot completely about the whole event. That was the extent of the "domestics" at our house.  It was a happy childhood.

I was determined that when I grew up I would make a difference. The most obvious way to accomplish that was to become a social worker and so I headed off to University to make it so. At the point of taking this in-home care summer job, I had a year under my belt toward my social work degree. I wasn't afraid. I was confident that I could step in and help this family, and many others for that matter. Armed with knowledge and practical advice, I packed my bag for my first 12 hour shift. What I didn't realize was that I would soon be on the receiving end of the lesson.

I had been briefed: three children (two pre-school and one in elementary), Mom has been given a diagnosis of fetal-alcohol syndrome compounded by a long history of drug and alcohol abuse. Dad was forcibly removed from the home the night before by the RCMP/ambulance; he was stabbed by Mom during a domestic. "Go in, help clean up and settle them down." These were my opening instructions.

I am not sure if any training could have prepared me for work that day, or quite honestly, for any of the days to come. Mom was physically injured, mentally exhausted and oddly hungry. The children were in chaos, running wildly without any awareness of my arrival. The 900 square foot house screamed of the turmoil this family had endured. From blood stained walls to clothes and toys littered everywhere, it was difficult to navigate the small space; the fridge was empty, the sink piled full and the stench of garbage strong. The only furniture was a couch and a TV on a small stand. There were no beds, no dressers or desks and no kitchen table. The question of what to *do* was bellowing inside my head.

I took a deep breath, pulled out the water bottle from my backpack and gently lowered myself to the floor. Tentatively, one by one, the family gathered around as if I was a strange animal invading their space. Gradually the conversation developed and from there the relationship began to grow.

Humility. But for the grace of God go I. Respect. This is what I learned. These were human beings. They were people with systemic multigenerational challenges so profound that I couldn't even begin to comprehend the complexity. We lived in different worlds. But because I was able to sit on the floor and put my fear, anxiety and righteousness aside, I was able to help. I didn't need to *do* anything at all. I just needed to *be*. This moment changed my life.

After a number of years as a social worker, I became restless and needed a change. The natural answer, at least to my husband, was law. So, I packed my bag, kissed my husband and headed off to get my law degree. He tended to be right about most things, so I trusted him. I am now grateful.

The job of a lawyer is fascinating. Each day I have the unique opportunity to meet ordinary people leading extraordinary lives. Most people think their lives are dull and routine, but spend some time with them. The personalities create the stories and often, real life is better than anything Hollywood could produce.

When I enter my conference room I am invited to personally participate in some of the biggest moments in the lives of my clients. It may be a divorce, a new house, a business venture, a death: all of the stories are unique and special in their own way. These are moments not likely to be soon, if ever, forgotten and the way the story flows is critical. The cast of characters add depth and complexity creating interesting and challenging dynamics, and I have discovered that no two stories are ever the same. My task is to help my clients complete the chapter but truthfully, my true role is simply to create hope. The practise of law is truly a privilege.

In these client meetings, I am amazed by the vibrancy and resolve of the ordinary person. Often people are faced with complex and difficult situations which for many would cause total shut down. Many times I believe that if faced with their same dilemma I would crawl into bed and never get out (of course that is never my advice). Remarkably however, these people often find the motivation deep within to walk through the problem. They navigate, with support, through the event and bring it to some kind of a conclusion such that they are able to move on. Sometimes the solutions are surprisingly simple - other times, intensely complex. Either way, a found resolution moves them on to their next chapter.

The many stories and experiences I have shared have become instrumental in helping others. I have found that the theories of social work and law have given me the framework, but the true answers are in the lives of the people I serve. Time and again, one person's story has given another the strength and courage to finish the chapter. Time and again, my clients tell me "you should write a book". Quite frankly, it seemed like good advice so I took it.

I find in business and in life, people are constantly seeking "the answer." I attend leadership conferences, business development meetings and the like and it seems as if everyone is trying to find out how to be bigger, better, smarter. And always there are theories and methods, just like at school, founded in research and study to help you advance. Often these theories and methods are helpful and provide a needed framework to move through a system. However, it is clear to me that more often it is the stories of the people that have the impact.

If you recall the last seminar you attended, I would guess that many would remember a particular human story that resonated. You might even remember smells, sights and sounds about the moment you heard that particular story as you were led to feel a certain way. The feeling could have been joy, sadness, fear or any range of emotions. But the story for some reason stuck with you and maybe somehow helped you advance a chapter. However, quite likely, you vaguely remember the theory behind it.

So in discovering your definition of success, it is my hope that the stories of others will help to inspire. These are not the stories of high-level corporate executives, movie stars or political leaders. While I am sure those people have many interesting stories to tell, these are the stories of ordinary people, leading what I believe to be, extraordinary lives.

It is my hope that in discovering these chapters you will take time to reflect on your own story and vision for your life. When you see your reflection are you happy? Are you where you want to be? Taking time to step outside ourselves and consider what really matters may open doors and new possibilities. A new perspective should always be welcomed.

If you feel stuck in the ordinary, allow the extraordinary to excite you. See opportunity in your story and have courage. Courage is required to make changes, accept new challenges or adjust a course. Recognize that allowing yourself time to bravely consider your options can sometimes make all the difference. Often, the risk is worth taking.

It is also possible that sometimes we look in the mirror, and for now, we are satisfied. Enjoy this moment too. You may be in your extraordinary and if so, soak it all up. There can be no greater success than to be truly fulfilled.

These are the stories of courageous ordinary people who have experienced and inspired the extraordinary. Their stories have graced my life. I hope they will do the same for you.

## 1

*In the world you will have trouble, but take courage, I have conquered the world.*

*John 16:33*

## CHOOSING WELL

My nine-year-old was thrilled to find out that she will have the ability to choose her own husband. She was sure that she would be assigned her life companion. In fact, she thought her Dad and I had already selected her mate and we were keeping this important secret locked away. I assured her this wasn't our plan (although I do understand that arranged marriages exist). She was delighted and then suddenly, overwhelmed. "How will I know who to pick?" she asked. Great question.

This was but one of the many intriguing questions posed by my daughters. How do we know when we find true love? How will we know we are dying? What job will be best for me? Where will I live when I grow up? And the list goes on and on. As a parent, it is difficult to know how to respond, particularly when we have similar questions ourselves.

Prediction is a game we all play. I suspect it has

something to do with our need for control and often our fear of change. Change is difficult, and for some it can be paralyzing. In my field of work change is a constant (and often a desired) result. However, many do not respond well to the challenge of adapting to change. In our expanding world there are many choices to be made and of course, choices can mean change. So how do we ensure we make the best choice?

There is no better way to learn to adjust to the pace of change and hone the skill of rapid decision-making than to become a property manager. As one of my side jobs, managing an apartment complex has taught me that nothing is constant and that although faced with seemingly unending and often monotonous decisions, your choices will matter. Learning to roll with the punches is essential to surviving the stress of managing those in transitional living.

When I first started this position, I was somewhat frantic and scattered in my approach. Dealing with so many lives at once, there was always a crisis. Suite 204 had a plumbing leak, Suite 306 was locked out and at the same time, everyone was angry with Suite 109 for a late night party. I would comfort and cajole tenants to arrive at a peaceful resolution. I would make choices on who would stay and who had to leave, who was granted leniency and who wasn't, and on and on it went. Also responsible for building maintenance, I would host all night painting parties with friends to ready apartments on a quick flip. I would jog at a quick pace while pushing the lawn mower in an effort to "speed-mow" after a long day at the office. Decisions were endless and fast; always juggling a dozen balls at one time. It was intense and I have no doubt I often looked ridiculous. Undoubtedly, some of my choices could have been improved upon.

However, despite my efforts to master control over this job by the many systems I put in place and the reminder notes I slid under doors, change was the only constant. Tenants would come and go and I was in a continuous cycle of starting over. I would screen and double screen tenants, hoping that by understanding their past I could predict their future in our apartment. But with each day new surprises came. I soon came to realize that in order to survive the position, I would have to simply accept that I had to work in constant flux. While an uncomfortable and unfamiliar place to be, accepting change as the norm allowed me to handle the job with a new calm.

I remember in particular one of my tenants named Stan, who struggled with addiction problems. He was a gentle man, but deeply troubled and unfortunately had burned bridges at most of the other housing locations in town. I took a chance and let him in, knowing full well that this tenancy would not be without a challenge. Taking time to get to know him, we developed a relationship and eventually he began to trust me and I, him.

We had ups and downs as he struggled with his illness. Relating with the tenants around him proved difficult and it was not unusual for me to be called in to resolve some type of dispute. However, one night I was called by a frantic tenant as Stan was pacing the hallways in his underwear carrying a knife. This was a new level. The neighbouring tenants were understandably upset. The police had already been called and so I immediately headed to the complex.

When I arrived, the police were ready to intervene. My tenant was confrontational on the surface, but I knew that beneath that exterior was a terrified little boy. He was being treated like a caged animal and so the typical fight or flight reaction was being invoked. I pleaded with the Constable in charge, asking only for an opportunity to speak to my tenant. The officer reluctantly agreed, moving himself and his partner slightly out of view but at all times ready in the event of a surprise.

I sat on the floor and called to Stan in a calm but authoritative manner. He was clearly under the influence of something and was visibly struggling to collect himself. After only a few short moments however, he recognized my voice and agreed to sit on the floor. Together we chatted as I convinced him to hand me the knife and wrap himself in a blanket. Eventually he consented to go to the hospital for help. We went with him to his suite and the depth of his illness became clear as I helped him gather his numerous bottles of prescription drugs.

With a huge sigh of relief and pleased with the end result I headed home. It was all in a day's work at the apartment complex. Stan was hospitalized for a time and in the days that followed he moved in and out of our complex, each time returning to what he considered to be a trusted friend. As a sign of good faith, he also referred his son as a new tenant.

His son, Bart, presented well. In his early 20s, he was recently employed as a general labourer and wanted to live close to his father. He was well aware of the mental health issues that had plagued his father as they both had been dealing with them their entire lives. Bart was a caregiver and this was a win-win from my perspective. We quickly signed Bart up to a lease.

Months passed and all was well. They lived in separate apartments and generally speaking, kept to themselves. One day, however, it was brought to my attention that Bart had not yet paid his rent and it was well past the first of the month. We started our usual process of calling and leaving notes and within a short time, Bart popped into the office to see me.

I remember this day so well. Bart was different. He was extremely agitated and as he sat before me I could see the beads of sweat forming on his forehead. I was clearly aware that something was terribly wrong and I immediately assumed that his dad wasn't doing well.

I was wrong. Bart himself was suffering intensely. He spoke about the pressure in managing his dad and trying to hold down a job at the same time. He was deliberate in his comments using strong commanding words so loaded with pain and frustration they were difficult to hear. Extremely frustrated, he felt that he was powerless; unable to have any type of control over his circumstances. Unpredictability and constant change were getting the better of him. He was empty.

Moving restlessly in his seat it took all my skills to settle him long enough that he would listen to a few suggestions for help. Drawing on my social work background, I recognized the crisis and attempted to outline some concrete steps to help him gain a level of control. Reluctantly he listened and quietly agreed that he would seek support. He was young with a whole life ahead. Hope was there for the taking.

Then, in a proud and strident way he announced he was short on cash, apologetic for the delay and insistent he would see me paid shortly. Without hesitation and recognizing his pride, I offered an extension on the rent and again strongly encouraged him to contact the resources I had suggested. Polite and confident in his departure, he quickly vanished. I had every reason to believe that the situation was on its way to a resolution.

A few days past and I still hadn't heard from Bart despite his assurances to remedy the outstanding rent. Although this type of delay was typical with some tenants, something here felt very wrong. Remembering our earlier attendance, I decided I would stop in at his apartment personally to speak with him directly. My caretaker also expressed worry that the suite had been abandoned since he hadn't seen any activity over the past few days. We decided to go to the suite immediately.

Together we knocked on the door. There was no reply. Using my master key, I unlocked the door and called out in a loud voice. Still no answer. We could see a light on in the corner of the one room and we entered.

Nothing would prepare me for what I saw that day. There in the room was a lifeless body; an image that will haunt me for the rest of my days. Bart had decided to take control in perhaps the only way he felt was possible. Overcome by what I understood he felt as uncontrollable change, he had decided to end it all. I was devastated. Bart was 22.

I now recognize that I was likely Bart's last contact prior to ending his life. I have replayed our conversation many times, wondering if my choices could have been different. And further, was there anything that I could have done to make Bart's choice different? Although this is an extreme example with obvious complexities, it is a daily reminder to me of the lesson that coping with change brings.

We must all learn to adapt to change and unpredictable circumstances such that the process of experiencing change does not negatively impact our life. It is different for everyone but at the same time, dealing with change is a universal experience. Drawing on the experiences of others can help us normalize the process and hopefully inspire us to use change to promote the positives. Knowing that we all feel uncomfortable in times of change can help us cope.

Each day I meet with people in varying levels of crisis, faced with choices that have the potential to have an enormous impact and often their choice will result in a substantial life change. Then at the end of my day, I go home to spend time with my daughters and help them develop the skills to make good choices and cope with the many changes that life presents. The opportunity to participate and influence on each of these occasions is both a privilege and a responsibility. Accepting also, however, that I don't always have control over the outcome is essential to my survival.

Bart's father has since disappeared into the world. I think of him often and hope that he is choosing well. Both he and his son have left a defining impression on my world. And while I recognize that Bart's outcome is an extreme reaction to change, I now have a new respect for the impact change can bring. While we need to embrace and encourage change in our lives, we also need to acknowledge that there can be a corresponding reaction, sometimes strong and unexpected. We must accept help along the way and recognize that we are not islands. We must be delicate with ourselves and respect our response. We must be kind to ourselves as we transition through life's changes, big or small and draw on the experiences of others to help us cope.

## REFLECTIONS:

1.  Take a moment to consider how you make choices in your life. What choices do you struggle with? What choices come easy? Examine how you feel, both physically and mentally, when choices are presented. What factors are important in making the decision? How do you choose?

2.  Reflect on one of your most difficult choices. How did you come to your decision? What impact did the process of choosing have on your life and the lives of others? What was helpful to you? What do you wish you could have done differently?

3.  Who do you support in making choices? How can you impact them in the most positive way? Are you able to accept the choices of others freely and without judgement? What matters in that process?

4.  Is there a future choice that you are considering? How will you make your decision? What factors are important? Who is impacted and how are you being supported in this process? Is there something you could do differently to help you to make your decision?

*For God gave us a spirit not of fear but of power and love and self-control.*

*2 Timothy 1-7*

## FACING FEAR: THE MAGIC OF MOTHERHOOD

You know that moment when you realize it is time to replace your bed sheets. There is a quiet moment of sadness; you have been comfortable for so long. You recognize that you spend a good portion of your day in that bed and, darn it, you deserve to be comfortable. But your current sheets are totally worn out. And so despite your sadness, you know you must make a change.

Then the fear sets in. Sleep is really important and you know that no matter what sheets you buy, you are going to be uncomfortable for a while. It will take time for the material to soften and feel like home. But you have to do it, you have no choice. You are compelled by your mother's voice reminding you of the importance of good clean sheets.

So you take the plunge. You buy new sheets. And despite all the promises on the package, they are itchy and uncomfortable. It doesn't feel right. And even though you know in time those sheets will be okay, your life is disrupted and you feel out of sorts. You have that nagging worry that maybe you made a mistake. Maybe you switched too early. Maybe you should have just kept the old sheets. You worry that maybe your bed will never quite feel comfortable again.

Eventually, however, the sheets soften and you can't even really remember what the old ones felt like. These new sheets become comfortable and again you settle into a restful slumber. It was worth the risk. After all, how hard can it be to transition to new sheets? Life is as it should be.

Living with passion is like buying new sheets. Throwing yourself into new and uncomfortable situations of all shapes and sizes, and challenging yourself to stretch. The rewards can be outstanding. But you have to allow yourself to be uncomfortable for a period of time before the new reality will feel like home.

Life is full of new and different opportunities and we are never sure where they will lead. Having the courage to face change can make all the difference. It is none of your business what other people are thinking or doing. You have only your own life to live and so the choices you make, while they will impact others, need to be choices that propel you forward in a positive direction. Sometimes a new experience, while exciting and fun, can also create feelings of fear. The experience of not knowing, while exhilarating, can also be scary.

Living with passion means living with energy. It means feeling invigorated by the newness. It also means that once the sheets start to feel to ordinary, you need to compel yourself to step out of your comfort zone and remake your bed. The possibilities are endless.

I agreed to take on a high school student for her work experience term. Everything was new to her. In our first meeting she proudly declared that she wanted to be a lawyer. Within moments, however, it was quickly apparent that she had no idea what that actually meant. We spent time discussing the role and as I spoke I saw a combination of both fear and excitement in her eyes.

You must walk into a room like you own it. You must at all times balance kindness and compassion with your duty to obtain the truth. You must find a way to make people feel comfortable enough to tell you their darkest secrets and you must at all times hold those secrets in confidence. You must take a complex set of facts, place them within a web of laws and then explain it all in plain language. You must put forth your best argument even when you know it is weak. You must recognize when to speak and when to be silent. You must pause. You must comfort and provide hope, while at the same time keeping your eye on the clock. And in the end, you must shake the hand of your opponent.

You will run into clients, opposing parties and the lawyer for the other side in your daily life at the grocery store, at your doctor's office, at your child's school or at a social events, and you must put it all behind you. At times it will be awkward. You must ignore this and be natural. You must respect people and their right to maintain a position, even when you disagree. You will know too much and have strong opinions. You must learn when to express them and you must be effective every time.

To do it all well, you must be fearless.

There is no class at law school that teaches you to be fearless. Nothing prepares you for the moment when you walk into a room and must not only hear the story but also have the solution. You must discover it all on your own. And so, in helping my young student begin to develop her skills, I encouraged her to engage in a life of firsts. Be courageous and try to step out of your comfort zone, I recommended. Conquer new things. Ask questions. Be interested. She appeared ready to climb Everest as she left my office. Time will tell.

As a mother, I know fear. From the moment you discover life inside you until, I suspect, the day you cross through the pearly gates, you will know fear as a parent. Every parent has this constant ache inside, and although the precipitating cause of the fear changes over time, the feeling remains the same.

My first legitimate bout of parenting fear came early. I was 27 weeks pregnant with my first child and had just enjoyed a fun-filled weekend away with my husband. It was now Monday morning and time to shift gears. My husband had an early departure, as his survey crew would be heading out on the road early for their next job. I jumped into the shower and started to plan the day ahead.

I was half-way through my shower routine when suddenly I felt very weak. The room started to close in around me. Dropping to the ground, I somehow knew I had to act quickly. I crawled out of the shower to my kitchen and pulling the phone cord to drop the phone to the floor, I quickly dialed my parents.

My dad answered the phone and I abruptly announced something was very wrong. I requested they come immediately. He asked no questions and hung up the line. I then fainted.

The next moment I remember is seeing my parents both hovering over me on the floor. "Is it coming?" my Mom asked. "Is what coming?" I wondered. "The baby. Is the baby coming?" Although it was my first experience at this whole child-birth thing, I was quite certain there was no baby coming. "No." I calmly stated. My dad sighed in huge relief, mostly because he was in no way prepared to deliver his grandchild.

Next question. "Well" said Mom with a frenzied

tone, "What is the number for 9-1-1?"; a question that would be told at dinner parties for years to come. And soon thereafter, the ambulance was on its way.

After numerous assessments the medical team recognized that special attention was required. I was soon taken by ambulance from our small hospital to the University hospital, a three hour drive across what seemed like endless railway tracks and large bumps. Once there, I was put under observation by order of the on-call physician since all obstetricians had gone home for the evening and I was clearly not in labour. I later learned from the staff that the nurses paced outside my door all night watching my health deteriorate, helpless.

When the obstetrician arrived for morning rounds, my condition was grave. I was rushed for surgery where it was discovered (as I understand it), that the back of my uterus had split opened and I was bleeding internally. Both my life and the life of our unborn child were at risk. In this medical miracle (as they later called it), they took the uterus out of my body with my child intact, flipped it over, fixed it, and put it all back in. We were the talk of the hospital.

I then spent three months in that hospital on bed rest. Each day brought new medical challenges, as my doctors struggled to bring me to term. I was warned and educated as informed consent was required for the many life-saving procedures. I was constantly being bombarded with shocking information. The moments in that cold sterile room were filled with anxiety.

My initial nurse mistakenly told me the baby had died. The next told me I would be forced to deliver. The messages were unclear and beyond difficult. My capacity to understand was compromised by pain and powerful medication. Truly in my initial days in ICU, I wasn't even clear where I was let alone the fact that I was pregnant.

The days of recovery were grueling and uncertain. The baby will likely be blind, deaf, developmentally delayed. Heart problems for sure. Dental will be impacted. Mobility compromised. This means potentially that and that means potentially this. On and on it went. Each day a new practitioner would arrive outlining the challenges ahead as I laid helpless trying to keep it together. Swarms of medical students would stand by my bed contemplating action. Hours of puzzled looks staring at me and wanting access to what was no longer private. Fear was an understatement.

Sanity was only maintained because of that little person growing within. She was determined from the get go. And just when I would start to lose the faith, she would kick me hard (often in the bladder) as if to remind me of my task. A force from within for sure. She wouldn't allow the fear to take over, even in my most difficult moments. And so my resolve grew strong and I was determined to produce a healthy child.

We were allowed to choose the day of delivery. So we chose a day filled with meaning for our family. We chose the day her great grandparents were killed in a car accident. A day of intense sadness transformed into a day of new life. A miracle. A celebration of lives. Our whole family rejoiced with the news, and stood ready to greet this little life.

The room was filled with physicians wanting to be present to witness this miracle birth and curious as to the condition the child would be in given the protracted issues and constant medical intervention over the previous months. They even allowed a photographer into the room to capture the moment. The medical team, while cautiously optimistic, weren't sure what challenges would lie ahead for both myself and my child. Quite frankly, they weren't sure either of us would survive the delivery.

I went in fearless. I was determined to not only survive, but to deliver beyond their expectations. I was literally filled with courage. In my mind, it was the beginning of a great story and I would declare her arrival, not whisper.

To everyone's surprise and delight, she was beyond perfect. The room erupted in cheers and my husband and I wept with gratitude. Totally healthy and completely developed, our girl took what she needed to be complete.

The doctor that held her during that most delicate

initial procedure later came to my recovery room. With tears in his eyes he retold his part of the story; his life forever changed by this remarkable moment. He honoured our family with wishes of continued health, as he noted my persistence and courage through a very difficult and troubling time. He acknowledged my fearlessness. I gave her all the credit.

A fulfilled life complemented by energy and passion will not be without fear and uncertainty. It is how we define and understand those moments that will determine our success. We must make a practice of buying new sheets. We must put ourselves out there and be uncomfortable. For in doing so, the new normal has endless potential.

I continue to face fear daily, both as a parent and as a lawyer. But there continues to be a strong internal kick that propels me forward. I have decided to be comfortable with being uncomfortable. I have decided that in this life I will not whisper.

## REFLECTIONS:

1. What role has fear played in your life?

2. How have you been held back by fear? Are you currently on hold?

3. Consider your process to overcome fear. What are your steps to break down fear? What is the worst that could happen if you move forward? What is the best that could happen? Are the fears rational or irrational? What could be your first step? How will you decide to move forward? Are you ready to be uncomfortable?

4. How do you react when you see others struggling with fear? How could you be more helpful?

---

## 3

*May God Almighty bless you and make you fruitful and increase your numbers until you become a community of peoples.*

*Genesis 28:3*

## INVESTED WITH INTEREST

I always knew that becoming a lawyer meant that I would need to develop a taste for scotch. You simply will not be taken seriously at an afterhours business meeting if you order a fluffy drink. I wanted in on the real conversations and I was sure that scotch was the answer. I was confident that someday scotch would be a great connector.

Obviously this required a plan. I convinced a good friend to join me in a vigorous training regime to accomplish this important task. Once a month we would get together, research a new flavour and develop an understanding of the particular brand. Initially, we struggled to choke down the shot, but eventually we looked forward to that first sip and savoured the moment. It didn't take long and we were self-proclaimed scotch drinkers.

We would record our thoughts in our "scotch journal" which, for security purposes, was cleverly disguised by my daughter's discarded Tinkerbelle journal. It was secured by a tiny little lock that held the stories of those many scotch adventures and on nights of a particularly enjoyable brand, the entries had a tendency to become quite racy. The Tinkerbelle journal held secrets of utmost importance. In fact, ultimately the journal will be buried with the first one of us to die. Secrets preserved. After only a few short months of scotch club, I understood very clearly why this smooth beverage was poured liberally in the back rooms of business meetings between trusted parties. Scotch has a tendency to strip you down to the bare honest truth.

Over time, my friend and I began to include "invited guests" in our club. We started first with my husband, slowly expanding to close friends and other interested participants. Scotch night became quite the event in our small town as different people requested an invite. More than a few business deals blossomed and doors were opened as a result of our quaint little club. Scotch became a great connector, an easy topic of discussion at networking events and in moments of delicate application, an honesty potion among close and trusted friends.

What I have come to realize, however, is that beyond the borders of my small town there exists one enormous worldly scotch club with numerous anonymous participants. Membership is identified by a simple but genuine invitation to partake, and from there a door is opened and the scotch drinker is warmly welcomed. It would seem that mastery of this important beverage grants you honourary access into the backroom of the business world. I was right: Scotch is a great connector.

I was attending a professional women's business development conference in the city with a couple of my good friends. The lunch break was "on our own" so as three girls with a child-free moment, it goes without saying that we grabbed a quick bite and headed straight to our favourite shoe store. Needless to say, we were late returning to the conference.

Our tardiness meant that we lost our table at the back of the room. Our only option was to head straight to the front of the room, all during the opening presentation of the keynote speaker. As discreetly as we could, we made our way to the front acutely aware that we were disruptive. The speaker was highly animated and captured our attention immediately with his vibrant stories and explicit language. Despite our efforts to be invisible, we were irritatingly noticeable. Once seated we quickly regained composure and joined along listening to what turned out to be a highly compelling speaker.

His message was all about women working in a men's world; how to survive and thrive. The speaker, a man, was not only an advocate for women in business and a professional business coach, but also enormously successful himself in his own entrepreneurial ventures. Within minutes of the presentation I knew he was someone I needed to meet. I was restless in my seat as I contemplated how I could find a way to connect.

But then, alas, the door opened. As part of his presentation he ran a short competition by which one person at each table could win a free hour of coaching. Determined and confident, I positioned myself for the win and captured it with ease. It was then that I developed my plan.

At the conclusion of his presentation, he sat alone at an adjacent table to watch the final presentation of the day: "Dress for Success". As the speaker opened her comments outlining the importance of scarves, it was abundantly clear that this was not a topic of interest to this man. I motioned quickly for him to join us at the empty seat at our table which he promptly did. Then, with every ounce of courage, I told him I wanted to immediately redeem my coupon for a free hour of coaching and with no hesitation I invited him to join me and my two friends for a scotch. I had peaked his interest.

He paused. He was clearly taken back by my request. He clarified right away that I was a scotch drinker. Yes, I assured him I was and dropped the names of a few of my favourite single malts to prove the point. Instantly, as if I had yelled the password across the room, the back door to the business club opened. Membership in the secret club was confirmed with a small nod and despite the required exit, which involved the dramatic departure of three ladies leading the key note speaker out through the audience, he followed us through the back door. Scandalous indeed.

Much was accomplished in the hour that followed. He was brilliant and I knew immediately that I had much to learn from this man. The scotch had connected me to someone whom I truly believed had capacity to make an enormous difference in my professional life. He later agreed to take me on as a client. As my business coach, he has opened more doors and championed my efforts in ways that have led me to tremendous success. I will forever be grateful for that single malt.

I clearly recognize that there are other ways besides an offering of alcohol to achieve connection. Scotch has just been one connector that has worked for me. The important message is that sometimes you need a great connector to open a door. In business and in life, opportunities are lost because people are unable to quickly identify a connection. In a fleeting moment possibility disappears.

Perhaps even more important, however, is that once that initial connection is achieved you must become interested. Truly interested. You must really want to know something about that other person. You must have an inner curiosity that pushes you to ask the less obvious questions. You must not be scripted or rehearsed. You must be genuine.

Being interested is a lost art. While such an obvious requirement of any conversation, the art of being interested is so often overlooked. We live in a world of distractions where busy is a badge of honour and as a result many of us are constantly multi-tasking and skipping on to the next thing. It is critical to achieve focus and be in the moment. Much is lost if your mind is elsewhere, and despite what you may think, your distraction is obvious. People know if you are not interested.

One of the most admirable qualities a person can possess is the ability to make others feel valued. When you speak to them, they listen. They inquire and are genuinely interested. It is not about going through the motions. Some people have the ability to make you feel like you are the most important conversation of their day. They care and it shows. This is a true skill. This is a skill that I see in highly successful and content people.

For many though, that first connection is achieved but then the interest requirement does not follow. The obvious cocktail party questions are attempted but then the conversation quickly dies. Awkward silence ensues. For some, a new connection means a race to collect the business card; for others an opportunity to spew copious amounts of inappropriate information about themselves. But true and valuable connection means taking the time to first find that spark and then develop it into a robust fire. Sometimes you can hit it off right away and instant flames emerge. Other times, you must gently and delicately work at the spark to find ways to draw the fire out. But the art of conversation involves both listening and sharing, openly and honestly, respecting and valuing the person opposite. So simple. Immensely rewarding. Totally attainable. Focus.

## REFLECTIONS:

1. What is your great connector? How do you open doors?
2. What are the benefits that connection brings to your life?
3. When connection is achieved, are you attentive? What helps to focus your attention? Are there ways to make the experience more successful?
4. What connections could you achieve to help you advance your purpose? What opportunities are there to make that happen? What will be your next steps?
5. How do you help others connect? Are there ways that you could help advance the purposes of others?

## 4

*I know your deeds, your love and faith, your service and perseverance, and that you are now doing more than you did at first.*

*Revelation 2:19*

## SERVANT LEADERS IN AN OVERWHELMING WORLD

In about 1945, the United Nations formulated *The Universal Declaration of Human Rights*[1] which was the first global expression articulating the inherent rights to which all human beings are entitled. It was adopted by the United Nations General Assembly on December 10, 1948. There are 30 Articles in the Declaration. Article 29 is remarkably insightful.

### Article 29

(1) Everyone has duties to the community in which alone the free and full development of his personality is possible.[2]

---

[1] United Nations., General Assembly. (1952). *Universal declaration of human rights. Final authorized text.* New York: United Nations Dept. of Public Information.

[2] *Ibid* at 8.

Article 29 means that everyone has a responsibility to the place we live and the people around us. The Declaration recognizes that only by watching out for each other, can we become our best selves. Article 29 means service.

Interesting that service is identified as a basic human right. Service as a right seems odd. It is easy to understand the responsibility, but a right that should be protected and treasured? With all the grumbling at my house to keep the house tidy, I'm not sure the service of others is always seen as a right.

However, if you think about the last time you engaged in the true service of others the concept becomes clear. You likely enjoyed that warm, pleasing moment where you felt good for giving back. And if you did it for all the right reasons with no expectation of compensation, it was likely extremely gratifying. In fact, the reward you received likely far exceeded any monetary value. In recalling this feeling it is not difficult to understand that for the good of all the act of service should form a fundamental human right.

My Mom was big on service. A firm believer in Article 29, any opportunity she saw for herself or her children to get involved was quickly taken. I delivered meals-on-wheels, visited the dying, prepared funeral lunches, picked weeds and shoveled snow, but to name a few. Our family was a quick yes and time was always made available to contribute. As a kid, I too grumbled and moaned heading out the door but the mood quickly changed as I engaged in the activity. Even as a young child, it was highly fulfilling to give back.

Service teaches us that life isn't always about you. We all get caught up from time to time navel gazing and according to my Mom, no good can come of it. In our busy, stressed and overcommitted world, free moments are often spent engaging in self-pity. We feel sad, jealous, envy. We hate our bodies. We struggle with change. We want more for ourselves but can't for the life of us figure out how to get it done. We have guilt, remorse, anxiety. The negativity is never ending.

Fortunately, we always have the healthy stream of positive motivation pouring through our Facebook feed to fill our minds with hopeful and pleasant thoughts. However, while warm and fuzzy, it is unlikely these moments will extend far into the future or result in any action. The true solution to navel gazing is found in exercising your fundamental human right and engaging in the service of others. In this positive act there exists true and pure joy.

When my clients are overwhelmed with their own world, I quickly encourage them to seek a volunteer opportunity. They think I am crazy. But step out of your world and into someone else's, just for a moment, and you can bring new understanding to your situation. It doesn't have to be a spectacular moment; a simple act can often bring the same level of reward. Service can be defined differently for everyone, depending on your time, talents and desire. The result of engaging, however, can be an opportunity to refocus and regain perspective. It can be a chance at a fresh start.

I have enjoyed the opportunity to work with many amazing people in my career, but one extraordinary man stands out when I speak of service. Growing up by extremely modest means, he had the intense desire to be and do great things. He is humble and gracious; a true gentleman in every sense of the word. However, fiercely determined, he overcame many obstacles throughout his lifetime to grow his estate to a substantial size. It wasn't easy, and when I spend time with him I learn about the kind of risks he had to take to arrive at his abundant wealth. I am in awe as I sit quietly and listen to him describe his journey, ever aware of that spark in his eye when he details those moments that matter the most.

He approached me one day with a desire to give back. He was a large contributor to established charities, however he found himself at a point where he wanted to do something more personal. In his 7th decade, his next business plan was to create a private foundation.

I worked with him over the course of a year to

establish the roots of this foundation. We spent a great deal of time talking about what he hoped to achieve through this gift and it was clear that he wanted to build something that would have an impact long into the future. He believed in the power of youth and he identified them as the best "bang for his buck." As a result, he decided to create a scholarship fund.

In order to bring publicity to the foundation we chose to host a public launch. Working with the schools, we sought out a handful of high school students that would be likely recipients. We asked them, as a favour to the foundation, to trial run our application software and help us streamline the process. These students were quick to oblige. It was an opportunity to be a part of something bigger; something truly meaningful. They believed they were doing a service.

When the public launch was set, we invited these students to be guests of the event in order that we could publically thank them for their contribution. They all quickly committed to attend. A few days later, I called them and requested they invite their families and maybe wear something nice. I gave very few details and they didn't seem too concerned.

What we didn't tell them is that in attendance at this event would be many honoured guests including the Deans of the Colleges they planned to attend, high profile politicians and other influential leaders. Seated on the stage with our Founder together with other distinguished guests they were personally introduced to everyone. They were delighted and grateful for the opportunities this introduction presented. But we didn't stop there.

From the podium I read the bios of these students to hundreds of their fellow classmates as well as teachers and community leaders in attendance. Calling them forward to formally be acknowledged by the Founder, I proudly announced that they were recipients of their requested scholarships (some in very sizeable amounts that would be more than enough to cover their entire year of expenses). They were stunned. Camera's captured their delight while simultaneously we filmed the pride and excitement of their families. It was a powerful and inspiring moment.

What was most remarkable, however, was the reaction of my client. For him it was a private quiet moment of deep fulfillment. Anyone who knew him could see it in his eyes. He had donated millions to charities in his lifetime and never had he experienced this reaction. This was different. The knowledge of the impact he had made for these individual students was unforgettable and the hope he had created was alive and vibrant.

What was most interesting was that the money, while important, wasn't the focus at all. The student that received a small scholarship was as impacted as the student who received the largest amount. They were all equally inspired by his story of success and his drive to succeed. It was the opportunity he was giving them, the potential he saw in them and the fact that he believed in them that hit them so hard. Truly, it was the recognition and the acknowledgement of a dream.

To my client, it was personal and gratifying. His life was forever changed in an unexpected moment of pure joy; a priceless reward. The results of his generosity will change lives in a profound way far into the future as these students, and many others, go on to graduate and serve their communities. Article 29.

## REFLECTIONS:

1.   What does service mean to you?
2.   What are your gifts? How can you employ them for service.
3.   Do you have a new or future opportunity to serve? How can you make a plan to give back in a meaningful and abundant way?
4.   How does the act of service grace your life? Are there challenges? Obstacles?
5.   How can you lead others to a life of service?

*Therefore, as God's chosen people, holy and dearly loved,*
*clothe yourselves with compassion, kindness, humility,*
*gentleness and patience.*

*Colossians 3:12*

## EMPATHIC ENERGY

Cheese snacks. The slogan for this treat should be "a highly traceable snack". When you eat them they leave that orange residue on your fingers and, well, everything else they touch. It's hard to hide a love for cheese snacks. They give you away every time.

My grandmother loved cheese snacks. She always had a bag in her cupboard ready for any emergency. A thrifty Ukrainian woman, she loved their salty goodness and kept close track of her inventory. There were other delicious snacks in the pantry above the cellar door, but the cheese snacks were one snack we knew not to disturb. A snack of cheese snacks required informed consent.

When my grandma was in her 95th year, we started to see a decline in her mental status. She had suffered many losses in her life, most recently the devastating loss of my mom, and as a result her ability to continue to live alone was gravely impacted. My dad and I moved her into the closest nursing home and tried to warm her surroundings as best we could. Of course, this meant that we provided her with an adequate stash of cheese snacks.

Grandma adjusted reasonably well to her surroundings. She had her own room and we filled it with memories of home. Pictures of all of the grandchildren and great grandchildren adorned the walls, and although Grandma was nearly blind, she would have her visitors describe the pictures and then she would detail with pride the current status of their life. Although her physical body was failing, her mind was sharp in the early days in this new home.

Then something changed. When visiting one day we noticed an orange residue on Grandma's pillow case. We didn't think much of it at first. We simply assumed that Grandma was enjoying a late night snack. But the next time we came, the pillow was nearly orange and on closer investigation we discovered bags of cheese snacks stashed within the pillowcase and in other strange locations throughout the room.

We asked Grandma what was happening with the cheese snacks. Grandma immediately lowered her voice and instructed us to close the door. Then she whispered "someone is stealing my cheese snacks." Tempted to laugh, we resisted as we could see from Grandma's face that this was a real concern in her mind. She then told us how she had been maintaining an inventory and each day cheese snacks go missing. "Could it be that you ate them Grandma?" we gently asked. "No." She dismissed us, insulted that we would even suggest she couldn't manage her cheese snacks stash with total competence. She was certain that someone was stealing her orange delight and so she had taken it upon herself to secure the asset. Grandma was totally distraught.

We spoke independently with the staff and they assured us that there was no crime being committed. They suggested, as we suspected, that Grandma was experiencing the onset of dementia. She was deeply upset about the alleged theft and determined to capture the thief. We were concerned that an unannounced visitor would be greeted with a surprise and so all staff were alerted to the concern.

We had conversations with Grandma to try and calm the waters. We inventoried the cheese snacks. We assured her that we would keep her in constant supply of cheese snacks, despite the alleged theft. Nothing we said made Grandma feel any better. It was the principle of the matter that had Grandma upset. She lost trust. She lost sleep. She lost cheese snacks.

On our long drive home, my Dad and I brainstormed ways to help Grandma. Dealing with irrational thoughts was difficult and finding a way to help Grandma did not prove easy. We thought about what we would want if we felt someone was stealing a prized possession. We talked about her helplessness and her feelings of loss of control. We tried for a moment to step into her shoes. Then it came to us.

We arrived the next day with a small portable safe. We inventoried the priceless snack with great care, providing a written count to be inserted into the safe. Then we locked away the cheese snacks into the safe and Grandma pinned the only key onto her undergarments. Grandma sighed with relief and we were amazed by the instant transformation. Again, she could enjoy restful sleep, uninterrupted by the endless crunch under her pillow. There would be no more orange hair. Grandma was at peace. In fact, in no time at all the cheese snacks became a non-issue and grandma was again able to enjoy sharing the proud stories of her offspring.

What did we learn?  We learned that this petty, trivial issue was very real to Grandma. Even though the problem seemed silly and somewhat funny, it caused her great consternation. We had to take it seriously. And it wasn't the issue itself that was so important, but rather, the solution needed to resolve a whole array of other complicated matters. We needed to respond in such a way that Grandma felt respected. We had to look behind the problem and then discover the answer at Grandma's level. We needed true empathy.

We must be humble helpers. We must walk in the shoes of others before we can offer our advice. Help is only that if the receiver is open to your suggestion and care must be taken to ensure that we are truly listening and open to the call. When we are open and responsive, we can enjoy the role of problem solving with all that this leadership role provides.

One only needs to spend time with a young child to understand the concept. Often, toddlers do not want any help but you know very clearly that they need it. "I do it myself", they will announce with determination and pride. But you will know full well that they do not have the skill or often dexterity to accomplish the task at hand. It is only when you help them in a way they wish to receive it that they will welcome your leadership. And often, they will be amazed by your skill and interested to learn your technique. Only, however, when they are ready and often that moment is clear.

As a lawyer, presenting the options to clients is a delicate matter. Many times clients do not want to hear what we have to say. Many times the news is not good. But we are paid to deliver the truth with pragmatism and honesty. And so making sure they are in a frame of mind to be open and receive help is critical to a positive outcome. Delivering a message in ways that clients can understand is of key importance. Many times, inviting support when necessary may make all the difference. Finally, finding solutions that a client can live with or implement is the only way the help will be truly fruitful. Helping is not about you. Make it about them.

When called upon, you must settle into the role of helper. With patience and compassion you must examine the issue from all angles. Tweak and tune until you reach the full clarity of a satisfactory outcome for all. The solution must be one that aligns with their needs, not yours. Let them own it and you shall enjoy all the rewards of giving.

## REFLECTIONS:

1.   When asked to help others, do I truly recognize and acknowledge the type of help they seek? Can I identify the best solution to meet their needs?

2.   How do I show true empathy? How does my empathy change in different situations?

3.   Are there times when it is more difficult for me to be empathic? Why?

4.   Are there areas in my life where I seek the empathy of others? How do I need to be heard?

5.   What happens when I do not feel heard? How do I respond? What is my role in clarifying my needs?

## 6

*Do not withhold good from those to who it is due, when it is in your power to act.*

*Proverbs 3:27*

## AND THE WINNER IS...

I clearly remember that special moment in kindergarten when I received my first red ribbon at track and field. It was a scorching hot day and children everywhere were juiced up on red licorice and McDonald's orange drink. I was wearing a green and orange velvet short set: it was warm, but yet incredibly stylish. As kindergarten students, we spent much of the day playing fun simple games like bounce the ball with the parachute and freeze tag. However, in my mind these games were a royal waste of my time and they had nothing to do with the real sport of track and field. I had been preparing in the park across from my house for weeks prior to this big day and having watched my brothers at track for a number of years I was well aware that there was only one event that truly mattered on this important school day. My focus was squarely on the relay race.

Finally, the last event of the day arrived. My team was set. We were given a few minutes to discuss our strategy and we took advantage of the time to practice passing the baton. From my worldly experience I knew that a dropped baton was fatal and mastering this skill would be key to our success. My teammates and I discussed our best runner order, analyzing our options closely to ensure optimum performance. We were clearly in it for the win. A vote was cast and I was nominated to close the race.

Ready, set, go: I waited impatiently and cheered as the baton was passed to the first, then the second and finally the third runner. I positioned myself for the exchange; the race was tight and I knew full well that a win now depended entirely on me. With the grace of Olympic athletes, my friend and I skillfully transitioned that mighty stick. I switched into high gear and ran like my life depended on it. Bursting across the finish line with every ounce of power I had in my tiny body, we were declared the winners!

In a few short moments we were handed our red ribbons. It was glorious! Glancing through the crowd, I saw my proud parents standing by to catch the end of the day. I was on top of the world!  The recognition I felt for achieving this tremendous feat was undeniable. It was in that moment wearing my orange and green velvet that I realized anything was possible.

We all have a need to be recognized. For some, public recognition is favoured. For others, it is the quiet recognition of a spouse, a child, or a friend that makes all the difference. Never being noticed however, is unacceptable.

As a young girl, I wanted to be noticed. Like other teenage girls, hours were spent learning make-up and hair tricks all designed to gather attention. How hard we all tried to be unique, but yet looking back at pictures, I realize now how similar our unique looks actually were. It didn't matter though, we were striving to be seen and heard.

Today I see that behavior repeated in my young daughters. As pre-teens they are trying so hard to find their own look and decide who they should be with the never-ending goal of simply wanting to be noticed. At a young age, a compliment is always welcome but a certificate or even better yet, a trophy can carry great weight. It is obvious to see that when a child is recognized for an accomplishment or uniqueness, a new confidence will follow which sometimes may even lead to a new or previously unexplored life direction. Many times, a door is opened.

The desire to be recognized does not change as we enter adulthood. In fact, for many it seems to intensify. In my business, I often see the sad results of a lack of recognition or perceived recognition. Much of the dysfunction and heartache I witness in my law office comes from clients who have felt unnoticed or unappreciated in an area of their life that to them held great importance. For example, matrimonial clients often are desperately sad that their partner doesn't notice them anymore. After many years of marriage, they have grown apart and forgotten what they loved so much about one another in the beginning. The only option, in their mind, is divorce. And for some, a budding new romance where recognition abounds advances the divorce process at a furious pace.

On other days I see business clients ever-hopeful that their business partner will recognize and acknowledge their hard work and contributions. A business partnership holds many of the same characteristics as a marriage, and many dissolutions have occurred not because the business was failing, but rather because the partners have not recognized or acknowledged the contributions of the other.

One of the most difficult and prevalent scenarios happens in estates. Often adult children are terribly angry on the death of a parent and the family is perplexed by their raw emotion. However, we soon discover that the child felt that they were not recognized, loved or acknowledged by the parent in a way that the child recognized and this feeling is validated (in their minds) as we move through the estate process. Maybe they weren't chosen as an executor. Maybe the inheritance isn't "fair" or what they expected. Whatever the case, the grieving process is compounded and the estate process complicated as these unsettled feelings by the child are experienced, often in a very public way.

We are all screaming to be noticed and recognized

in some way. Sometimes what may appear to be the right recognition to the outside world, isn't the kind of recognition we are seeking at all. And other times, the most simple and quiet recognition changes everything. The type of recognition is different for everyone, but the overarching need to be acknowledged is universal.

I think of the many different ways I have been formally recognized in my life and the impact even those moments have had on my life.

In grade 7 we moved from our small Catholic school into the public system. It was a big "graduating" year for us, complete with an awards ceremony. There were numerous awards: best attendance, most improved student, highest marks etc. The last award however, was to be presented by the President of the Catholic Women's League (CWL) and the student was chosen by a school committee, which was comprised of parents, teachers and administrators. Once chosen, the student's name was provided to the CWL so that an actual plaque could be prepared. All the other awards got a simple certificate. This award was a fancy, shiny plaque with your name engraved.

The name of the award was "Student of the Year" and was presented to the student that demonstrated strong leadership skills and was respected by their teachers and classmates alike. It was a coveted award, and I was in a class of tough competition.

The President of the CWL came forward to read the bio of the winning student. I was as proud as ever, not even listening very closely to the presentation. Why? Well because the President was none other than my mom. I was so amazed to see her there in her fine suit speaking to my school and holding a very important and honourable role. In that moment of pride, I already felt recognized simply through my mom's success. That would have been enough for me.

It then goes without saying, that I was beyond delighted (and surprised) when my name was called to step forward and receive this prestigious award. For my mom, it was a moment of sheer pride. For myself, it was like I was receiving the Nobel Prize. Quite frankly, I believe the moment felt so much bigger for everyone in light of the circumstances. Watching my Mom glow as she proudly hugged me on stage in a very personal and touching way had a strong impact on everyone. Witnessing the reaction of the crowd, teachers later commented that parents around the room were hugging their kids a little tighter as they watched the presentation. The "Student of the Year" award itself seemed less important as parents quietly acknowledged their own children in this moment, giving each of us the recognition we so clearly desire from our folks. The room was filled with the acknowledgement of the pride of a family. As a result, the "Student of the Year" plaque still hangs proudly in my old bedroom at my parent's house as a reminder of this very special day. That presentation was a defining moment in my life in understanding the importance of recognition for all of us.

The following year a group of friends and I won the Attorney General's Award for Crime Prevention after developing an abduction awareness campaign for elementary students. I was oblivious. In fact, I almost didn't show up for the ceremony. The speeches were long and didn't hold much importance. There was little personal connection for me and as a result to this day, I have no idea where that plaque went.

University held its own moments of recognition. In my first year of University, I made the Dean's List (meaning an over 90% average). There were scholarships, elite clubs and special privileges attached to this achievement. None of it seemed all that remarkable or interesting to me and although I was grateful that doors were opening, I didn't feel that the recognition was all that necessary or remarkable.

However, one experience in my early university days had an enormous impact. I was in my Political Science lecture, a required Arts class that I needed to complete my undergrad. The professor was articulate and demanding and I enjoyed his class immensely although I will admit, I was totally intimidated. Our required paper was to detail the importance of the Rule of Law, a topic foreign to me prior to this class. On this particular day, we were scheduled to receive our papers back and the professor opened the class talking about how desperately sad the effort had been on this major assignment. He went on to express his anger in a strong and somewhat threatening manner, then softening somewhat by sharing his dismay and identifying ambivalence in the minds of our young people as the cause of this most recent disappointment. He was a passionate man and I had no doubt we had collectively failed him. Then, he paused. In his moment of silence I was frozen in my chair afraid of what was to come.

He then announced that there had been one bright light. One person who had captured the essence and meaning of the Rule of Law and he was so astounded by the quality of the paper that he wanted to take time out of his lecture to share. His lecture time was precious so we knew this was truly an extraordinary measure. The entire class sat up straighter in the chairs. He then began to slowly read from the paper in front of him.

Within moments I recognized the words coming from his mouth. I didn't know if I should crawl under the desk and sneak out of the room or leap down the aisle to the podium. I was both ecstatic and terrified in the same moment. When he finished, he proudly called out my name and asked me to stand. As I slowly rose to my feet, 150 classmates clapped and cheered. My professor took a long hard look at me, slowly walked up the steps of the theatre to my seat and handed me my paper without saying a word.

While I was nervous to receive this recognition it clearly ranked high on my list. Being noticed not only by a room full of university students, but better yet by a professor I highly respected, wasn't a moment I would soon forget. I will admit I was glad I wasn't wearing orange and green velvet.

Years later I applied to law school and I did it all in secret. When I finally gathered the courage to announce my acceptance to my parents, my mom being the true champion she was, jumped for joy. My dad however, a prominent lawyer himself, shook his head in dismay and said very little. In a moment where I felt I so deserved recognition, I was robbed. I didn't understand his reaction until a considerable time later.

It was only after my first year marks were released that my Dad came around. I was home, working at his firm for the summer months to gain experience and make a little spending cash. The marks were released and we could phone in to hear our results. My Dad gave me "the talk", explaining that law school isn't like any other school. I shouldn't expect the Dean's List, in fact, I better be prepared for the worst. He was pessimistic in his tone, and I felt the same anxiety as I did when my Torts professor pulled out the Socratic Method at our 8am lecture.

Terrified.

I went down to the privacy of my bedroom to receive what I was sure would be devastating news. I reached into my old white desk only to find a box of my pencil crayons and some paper shaped like a puppy. I dialed the phone and entered my student number. With a deep breath, I started to write the results on the puppy paper. I hung up the phone in disbelief and quickly redialed the number to repeat the process. I was sure I had made an error but strangely, the same information was relayed back.

I calmly walked upstairs where my parents and husband were anxiously gathered. One look at my white face and they were quick to reassure me that they loved me no matter the result. I handed the puppy paper to my dad. "Straight A's", I said, in a calm voice void of all emotion. They were astounded. In that moment, my dad recognized me not only as his accomplished daughter, but also as his esteemed colleague. I couldn't have asked for anything more.

To celebrate that night we went to the local Chinese restaurant. At the end of the meal, the fortune cookies were passed around. It has always been our families practice to each take turns reading them out loud. When I read my cookie I was stunned. It couldn't be true, this had to be a trick. I read the fortune to the group "You would make a good lawyer" it said. My family was as shocked as I was and assured me it wasn't planted. It was an amazing coincidence that this fortune was revealed and to this day is framed and hangs proudly over my dad's desk together with both of our graduating pictures.

It was at that time, my dad shared with me the reasons for his initial reaction to my announcement of law school. He had significant worries having been a practitioner for many years in what he considered to be a very difficult field for a woman. He expressed his strong desire for grandchildren and his hope that I would find a way to balance it all. He wasn't certain that this was possible. Little did he know that I would soon join him in practice and he would be changing diapers as a part of his regular day at the office.

Law school continued to be rewarding. I was presented with scholarships, great marks and ultimately graduated with Great Distinction (over 90% average). There were five of us out of a class of 110 to receive this distinguished honour. An affirmation of what I already discovered and a proud moment for my family, but in my mind, the recognition I needed had already been achieved.

My most celebrated public achievement to date would be receiving the Queen Elizabeth II Diamond Jubilee Medal for my work across the nation in palliative care. The medal is shiny and important and I was deeply honoured to be recognized at a public ceremony. But again, I felt I had received all the recognition I needed for palliative care when my mom died in my dad's arms in their home, after my brothers and I worked to create a supportive palliative care environment at her request. I know my Mom was grateful that this was the way her story ended and I felt, although silent and private, a very strong acknowledgement and recognition for all of us involved in her care. The bond that was created within our family as a result of this experience and the subsequent understanding of the need that all people have the potential to experience dying in this way was a form of recognition that pushed my life in a different direction. This experience spurred me into a course of advocacy that brought me to that shiny Queen's medal. I maybe didn't know that as I sat at my mom's bedside, but I certainly did when they pinned the medal on my lapel. Looking back, I understand now how those important moments of recognition changed my path and led me to a new place. They propelled me in a new direction and encouraged me to be the best version of myself. The right recognition changed my life.

## REFLECTIONS:

1. How do you define recognition?

2. Examine the times in your life you have been recognized. Was there a difference in your reaction? If so, what made the difference?

3. Are there times where you have been overlooked? How did this impact your life? What was your role in this process?

4. Do you offer recognition to others freely and without reservation? Are you attentive to their desired form of recognition? Are there barriers to delivering proper recognition? If so, is there a solution?

5. What recognition would you like to next achieve?

## 7

*Trust in the Lord with all your heart and lean not on
your own understanding; in all your ways submit to him,
and he will make your paths straight.*

*Proverbs 3:5-6*

## RECALIBRATING YOUR TRUE NORTH

My 12 year old daughter has a strong sense of
justice. Lines are crisp and clean in her world. She
isn't afraid to stand up for what she believes
regardless of the consequences. We first came to
recognize this when she was in kindergarten. A
group of girls decided to start a club but sadly
excluded one girl they deemed unworthy. My
daughter was appalled. So quickly and quietly, all
on her own, she started a different club; including
everyone but the three girls. Point made. When the
teacher called to tell us what had transpired we
could not have been more proud.

At the young age of 12 however, she has already
paid a price for being the voice of reason. She has
been bullied and excluded. There are nights of tears
and questions; sadness and fear. She can't
understand why people are so mean. She wonders if
she is making the best choice when the result is
often painful for her. She wonders why she often

feels so alone standing up for what is right. At 12, she asks me sweetly if it gets better, easier. And at 12, she already knows it likely won't.

As lawyers, we too must see clean lines. We must stand up for justice. We must zealously advocate for our clients, even when their choice is not popular. Of course, the most obvious question asked of a lawyer is how can you act when you know your client has committed a horrific crime. But ethical dilemmas are not only reserved for criminal lawyers. In my solicitors practice I am faced with difficult ethical dilemmas every day.

What if your client wants to engage in a public tender but asks you to privately exclude one group from the opportunity? What if you see your clients using unfair advantages or information to strengthen their position? What if you don't like your client? Don't trust them? Don't respect them?

Of course, our legal ethics guide us and provide a framework for resolution. In addition and lucky for me, I practice law with my father; a man with a clear and decisive code of ethics. The lines are clean for my father. And although the results of implementing the correct ethical decision may be difficult, the high ground is where he stands. In teaching me how to reach that high ground each and every time, my father has taught me the importance of the pause.

Reflection and time are the friend of a lawyer.

Working in an environment where every minute counts, it is difficult to slow down. However, we must pull time out of our busy day to pause and methodically work through scenarios to capture the answer. Decisions made in haste are often flawed. Knowing when to press pause is a learned skill for a lawyer.

Holding the letter one more day for reflection despite the client's hurried timeline, taking a message on a call so you perform the callback when you are prepared, stepping away and consulting a colleague for a second opinion; all examples of pauses that we as lawyers must remind ourselves to do regularly.

Pressing pause is a learned skill for everyone. Decision making is a life requirement and for many, a real challenge. Anxiety is the new epidemic as the rapid pace of our world forces people to advance further and faster than their comfort zones allow. Granting yourself permission to pause is a skill that can pull you away from the frenzy and allow the necessary time for you to make your right decision.

But the pause is just that, a pause. It is a moment, a shift, a gap. It is not a dead stop. And the result of the pause must be an active decision. Perhaps to do nothing, which in itself is an active decision. The pause, I tell my 12 year old, is not a never-ending display of indecision. You must choose something.

"Should I stay or should I go?" ask my matrimonial

clients. "Is it time to sell?" ask my commercial clients. "How do I make this decision?" asks my elderly client making final choices on her Will. Decisions are difficult.

I represent nurses who are facing disciplinary action. In a profession where decisions have significant consequences, it is a field ripe with ethical dilemmas. A clear code of ethics and policies exists contemplating endless scenarios in an attempt to streamline results. But nursing is a human experience, and despite the endless material, not every scenario has been contemplated.

A nurse I was representing was faced with a tough decision. A palliative patient whom she had worked with for an extended period made a simple request. He wanted his pain medication left by his bedside to take a few hours later than scheduled, allowing him a full night sleep. Such a simple, clean request.

He was a determined, strong willed man in his 60s. He was suffering intensely in the final stages of his cancer. Her shift was ending and overtime was not permitted. The only alternative was having the on-call nurse return to work later than night to hand this man two pills. Leaving the pills by his bedside put her career at risk.

Complicating matters, the man added an obstacle. He gave her an ultimatum. He said if she wouldn't leave the pills, he would go med-free all night. You see the man was aware that the on-call nurse had to drive 40 minutes from a neighbouring town in the dark of night in the dead of winter to hand him two pills. He had driven that highway many times in his life and even on a crisp summer morning it was dangerous. He would rather go without than force the on-call nurse to drive that rural highway and hand him two pills.

My nurse understood completely. No pain medication would mean unbearable pain and suffering.

A simple choice? She trusted the man. She knew he understood his medication and that he was capable of consuming the two pills. She wrestled with the idea both in her head and out loud in intense discussion with this dying man. His dignity was at risk. The fact was, if he was at home the whole bottle of pills would be by his bedside.

She decided to leave them. She placed them in a covered cup in a closed drawer beside the bed. He took them without incident. He was grateful.

Unfortunately for her, a colleague reported the decision and her job was at risk. The man died a few weeks later, never knowing the impact of his choice. She never regretted hers. However sitting teary-eyed before the Investigative Officer facing significant consequences, she humbly agreed to choose a different path if faced with this dilemma in future.

Her hand was forced. But she did make a decision

and walked through the consequences holding her head high. The fact that she actively made a choice has allowed her to move forward and carry on providing care to the sick and dying.

For many of my clients, moving forward is an unavailable path. They are paralyzed and incapable of making a decision. The results of their long standing uncertainty can be grave.

Sitting in indecision is torture and in my opinion, dangerous. Not choosing a path for yourself means someone else will. It means handing over your power. Not deciding is truly a form of giving up and with that, a lost opportunity. For these clients, health and wellbeing suffer exponentially and grieving is complicated.

If faced with indecision, you can make an active choice to do nothing. Constructive delay is a tactic used by lawyers regularly to force the other hand. Decide to do nothing. Choose to not respond. An active decision on a plan of action. Often, constructive delay is highly effective. The key, however, is that it is a choice. It is a decision with a preferred consequence. It is not a never-ending display of indecision. It is a decision following a pause.

My 12 year old faces big decisions ahead. She is just at the beginning of defining justice in her world. I will be there to help her find the high road. I will continue to teach her the pause.

## REFLECTIONS:

1.  We all make multiple decisions each day. What decisions are you currently facing in your life that are challenging you? Where are you at in the process of making those decisions?

2.  Are you skilled at making decisions? What decisions are easy? What decisions are difficult? What makes the difference?

3.  When faced with a difficult decision, how do you move forward? How do you break down a decision into manageable parts? When you are stuck, what helps you move forward?

4.  Have you ever consciously decided to pause? What was the result?

## 8

*In everything he did he had great success, because the Lord was with him.*

*1 Samuel 18:15*

## PROGRESSION NOT PERFECTION

How do you define success? For many success is related to finances; toys and a big bank account. For others, it is about the perception of a win; a contract, an award, a bonus. And for many others, it is described as security; peacefulness, time or freedom. There are many ways to define success and usually when asked, the answer is the big picture. It is a destination at the end of a long road.

However defining success in this way can be daunting. If success means only attaining the end goal, then for many, reaching that destination seems insurmountable. The result of this type of thinking is often self-doubt followed by paralysis and ultimately, defeat. If success is too far away, most will tire of trying or get frustrated with the journey and give up. Think of weight loss. If you are 100 pounds overweight and your goal is to drop four sizes and run a marathon - my guess is you might find yourself eating bonbons and using your treadmill as a place to hang your ironing. Success is simply too far away. Any good fitness instructor is going to tell you to break the process down into more manageable parts.

The definition of success needs to be broader than the end goal. The process needs to be broken down into smaller parts, but also with success viewed from different angles. Although this seems trite, in practice I am amazed at how often success along the journey is overlooked.

Most people are not very good at acknowledging small moments of success. Somehow these accomplishments seem insignificant, and people feel pompous or arrogant for taking time to pat themselves on the back. However, it takes many small steps of success to reach the ultimate goal and often times, the ultimate goal changes as the small successes are achieved. Many people focus only on the prize at the end, giving little or no credit to the bazillion pieces that had to happen to get them there. I believe that finding a way to force yourself to recognize, acknowledge and celebrate the small steps can not only be extremely gratifying, but can fundamentally change the way that you view your life. You may even find, that this process completely changes your direction.

When I was completing my social work practicum, I worked in a women's transitional home. The residents were woman who had moved from a temporary crisis centre to a secure apartment complex in order to have longer term support to help get their lives on track. These women had escaped horrific violence to arrive at this doorstep and most often, were wavering on their decision to return home. The goal of the program was to move them to a position of self-sufficiency in six to twelve months and to inspire motivation and confidence along the way.

I remember in particular a girl named Karen. She was 22 years old. She had two children and had escaped an extremely controlling and violent partner. Her physical scars had healed, but the mental trauma was fully intact. She was attractive, smart and presentable. I was sure that with some courage and sweat equity, we could quickly get her life on track. And she was more than willing to participate in the change.

In meeting with her and listening to her needs, it was clear that a formal education was required to help her become self-sustaining and maintain her family. She was excited about the chance. We spent hours talking about what motivated and interested her and ultimately, what she wanted to do with her life. As an eager social worker, it was easy to develop manageable, attainable and measureable goals. I was confident that Karen was going to be a huge success story.

We put all the pieces in place. I even arranged a full makeover with a qualified stylist friend. We toured the school campus and enrolled in classes, settled finances, found childcare and arranged transportation. She was ready to turn the page and all the pieces were in place. And Karen was genuinely excited!

First day of classes arrived. Karen wouldn't unlock her door. Despite my knocking, she wouldn't get out of bed.

Second day of classes arrived. No response from Karen. After a few gentle knocks I sat quietly outside her door and hoped she would find courage.

Third day of classes came and went. No Karen. I walked up to her door, turned around and went to my office. I did not knock.

Fourth day of classes, and I stayed in my office. Karen came out of her apartment to see me. She was in her pajama pants and an oversized sweat shirt. Her hair was matted and greasy; her skin pale. She told me that she had called the school that morning and dropped out. She wasn't going and she was adamant that nothing I said would change that. I was devastated. In my mind, she didn't even try.

Where did I go wrong? Were they my goals or her goals? Had I pushed too hard and set her back? We had come so close and she was so excited - how could it all change on a dime. All I could see was an epic failure. We never crossed the finish line - heck, we didn't even get out of the gate. How could there be any success here?

But Karen then confided in me. She told me it was the first time in many, many years that she had felt excitement and joy. Period. That was it. A fleeting but extremely important moment of pure joy. It was absolutely pivotal for her and in her mind, this was a moment of total success. Her emotional barometer had never advanced beyond neutral in *years*. Oh, she had felt terror, fear, pain, sadness, depression and everything in between in the range of negative emotions. However, what we had succeeded in achieving was helping her feel true joy and excitement. She was elated. And as far as she was concerned, that was enough success to last a very long time. She returned to her husband the next day.

Now, if you have an understanding of domestic violence, the ending to that story won't surprise you. Statistically it has been shown that people in those types of situations will leave many, many times before they make the decision to break away for good (if they in fact ever do). For someone on the outside looking in, it is a bizarre circumstance and can be incredibly frustrating to accept.

It took me a long time to accept this as a success. However, I have come to understand that for Karen, this small step was a total success to be recognized, acknowledged and celebrated. I have no idea whatever became of Karen but what I do know is that for a brief moment, we created hope.

When I worked child protection, my supervisor

understood the concept of acknowledging success better than anyone I knew. She ran a busy office, and with the social workers managing darkness every day, she spent a good deal of time being concerned about the mental health of the team.

On a particularly bad day, I remember her pulling me into her office to debrief the horrific tale of sexual abuse I had uncovered with my young client. Some days, it hit you worse than others and on that particular day, I was only able to see black as I described the contacts I had made not only with this family, but also with the 35 other families on my caseload. I was struggling with words and emotions; feeling like wave after wave was knocking me over as I described file after file, family after family.

She sent me home to rest. In the morning when I was refreshed, she came into my office with a bright cheery smile. She had a new assignment and couldn't wait to hand it over. She was almost giddy and I was completely dreading what was to come.

The assignment was simple. At the end of each day before I was allowed to leave, I was to provide her with details of two success stories from the day. If she wasn't there, they were to be in writing and left on her desk. She smiled sweetly and then abruptly kicked me out of her office to get to work.

I was a mess. How could I possibly find two success stories *every* day? At that point, I couldn't even give you one. Mission impossible. I was sure to fail.

But then I remembered Karen. I was reminded of how just even the feeling of joy for a fleeting moment was in her mind, a total success. I slowly and gently started to unravel my files and redefine success for my families - small, incremental and not necessarily typical. As I reviewed the stacks I started to see success everywhere. It was raining success! I was excited, and so I began to share the excitement with some of my families. Over time I began to teach them to identify success in their day; often acknowledging fleeting moments of feeling successful. We celebrated together and before I knew what had happened, my focus completely changed.

It is difficult to understand how truly remarkable this revelation had become. These were parents who had, for whatever reason, failed to protect their child from horrific abuse. Sometimes, the parents themselves were the perpetrators. The innocent children were physically or sexually assaulted, sometimes both; most often by people they trusted. These were families who were operating at extremely high levels of crisis with little hope of a stable existence. For many, survival itself was an insurmountable goal. Society, if they knew the story, would characterize many of these parents as monsters.

Most importantly, if I was unable to see through the situation to some level of success for the individual family, how could I possibly expect the families to rise out of the darkness in any way? There had to be a way to believe it was possible. It is understandable that if a well-adjusted family with a white picket fence was the end goal and the only definition of success, then failure was likely the outcome. We needed small successes along the way to pick these families up and move them to a place of healing and strength.

Oddly enough, at the end of my day I became excited to head to the office of my supervisor and detail the gem I had uncovered. "Mary got out of bed and made breakfast." "George was able to sit through one full class today." "John walked to the next room when he got angry and phoned me." It was remarkable. This simple task of honoring and acknowledging each small success changed everything. It is a practice I have continued in my daily routine since that time.

## REFLECTIONS:

1.  Consider the last few days and identify five moments of success. Did you notice you were successful in the moment? How did you acknowledge your achievements?

2.  Is it difficult to acknowledge positive moments in your life? If so, why?

3.  Do you see success in others? How do you help them recognize their achievements?

## 9

*And we know that in all things God works for the good of those who love him, who have been called according to his purpose.*

*Romans 8:28*

## GAINING PERSPECTIVE

In my law practice, I continue to be goal-oriented. People pay me well to get things done and help them achieve success. My business clients are often task driven and have a final destination in mind as they work on their ventures. From my perspective, helping them identify success along the way is critical.

Sometimes, however, we are called to pause and evaluate. Recently I had a very interesting experience that did just that. On Tuesday, I met with a man named Jake. Jake was 87 years old and was attending at my office to transfer property to his granddaughter. I had never met Jake before, and in fact, his granddaughter had made all the arrangements.

After our 45 minutes together the only word I would use to describe Jake would be curmudgeon. He was a grumpy old man. Jake was bitter.

He told me life was a total waste of time. As he said it, he sat on the word *total* for long enough that his message was abundantly clear. He went on to explain that nothing he did mattered and that he couldn't wait to die and let it be over. Although I suspect that Jake may have been suffering from some form of depression, it was not as obvious as you might think based on his demeanor. While his message was clear, he did not appear sad or despondent when he made the statement. He was calm and exacting in his delivery; particularly eloquent in his description of both his wasted life and, in his view, the desperate state of world affairs. In a strange way, he actually appeared happy to share his message of doom and gloom.

I then asked Jake if he had children. I was trying to move to a topic that surely would draw him out of his personal storm. Yes, he said, he had ten. He then proclaimed that having children was a total waste of effort and in his opinion, he would have been better off not having had any at all. I was dumbfounded. I had trouble finding words and struggled in an effort to avoid confrontation. Suddenly this all felt very personal and it was becoming difficult to maintain my professional distance. Part of me was desperate to end the meeting as I didn't want to get sucked into his dark vortex. Jake's resolute manner was nothing less than disturbing.

After detailing his disdain for my generations' efforts to destroy the world he specifically suggested that as lawyer and leader in the community I had a direct hand in the problem. To end the crescendo of mounting rage, his parting words were "wait until you are 87, you will understand exactly what I mean." Wow. I truly in that moment hoped I never would.

I left the meeting rattled. Could he be right? When I am 87 will this make sense to me? Will all I have strived for mean absolutely nothing? Clearly I didn't agree with him, but nonetheless I was shaken by his words. I left the office that night distracted and somewhat distraught. I felt terribly sad for this man (and incidentally, those were my parting words to him - which he immediately rejected and told me to save my breath). I felt worried for my future and for the future of my children. I was somewhat amazed also, that I had allowed this man's negativity to enter my core.

The next morning I awoke slightly troubled. Jakes words bellowed in my mind over and again. Alas, however, my work day commenced with a ray of light. My first appointment was Molly.

Molly was 87 (what are the chances of seeing another 87 year old the next day?) and was coming in to sign papers. It was to be a quick meeting as her niece was arriving from a fair distance to join her for a few days of visiting. Molly was anxious to return home to prepare for her arrival.

I met with her and we signed her papers. She

couldn't have been more opposite to Jake. Molly was polite and kind, and filled with gratitude that I had accommodated her request to quickly attend to paperwork that had been troubling her for some time. At the close of the meeting I asked Molly if she had time for one short story that I felt compelled to share. She obliged me graciously, despite her impending plans.

I told her about my meeting with Jake. As I shared my shock and disbelief at my interactions the day before, my eyes welled with tears and it was clear to Molly that I had been profoundly impacted by this man. She could see fear and desperation in my eyes and I described to her his disdain for life so intense that he even regretted having ten children. Every part of me was begging her to tell me life wasn't so dire and that Jake was basically a lost soul.

Contrast Jake with Molly. Molly was never able to have children, although she desperately would have loved to have one if not ten. She was married to the love of her life who died 2 weeks before their 50th wedding anniversary. She described him so vividly that I felt I knew him for as long as she had. Molly worked hard throughout her lifetime, both physically and mentally. She was a farm wife dependant on the sky for survival and grateful for all that the land had provided. Sadly, only to become widowed a few short years after retiring and moving to the city to start life anew. There was no opportunity to enjoy with her life partner, the spoils of their labour. Life had been hard, but Molly was grateful and her beautiful spirit shone through. She was in fact, in my office to sign her Will gifting her estate partly to her small country church to help maintain the cemetery for friends that had passed on, and partly to be shared between her many nieces, nephews and godchildren in the hope that her gift would help ease a burden for them. She was a true inspiration.

 She looked straight into my eyes and assured me that worry would do me no good. She said I was right to feel sorry for this man and that a spirit of kindness and gratitude will lead me to the right answer when I myself turn 87. Molly was indeed, in her soft spoken way, very wise. She told me, that in a strange way, she could understand this man's sadness and anxiety. Molly empathized with his pain and with grace she explained how the dramatic changes witnessed over the last 87 years have caused her pause on more than one occasion. Molly identified her greatest and most important success as having quality relationships with all kinds of people in many walks of life. She closed saying she would pray that he finds peace in his heart, hugged me and left my office. On that day, I gained tremendous perspective. And on my 87th birthday, I plan to think of Molly.

## REFLECTION:

1.  What do you want your 87 to look like? What will be your greatest accomplishment? How will you know you will have fulfilled your purpose?

2.  Are you on track to have a life that you can look back on with gratitude?

3.  Are you Molly or Jake? What changes or decisions might change the picture?

4.  Do you know a Molly or a Jake? How do you feel when you think about them? Why?

## 10

*One who loves a pure heart and who speaks with grace
will have the king for a friend.*

*Proverbs 22:11*

## CHIN HELD HIGH: THE COURAGE OF ACCEPTANCE

Last week the front page of the newspaper led with devastating news. A farming family lost their three young daughters (a nine year old and twins of eleven years old) in a farming accident. The young girls were playing on the back of the grain truck (which undoubtedly, like other farm kids, they had done hundreds of times before) when they fell in and were smothered by the grain. Despite the parent's frantic efforts to get them out, all three children died. Left surviving in this tormented family were the parents and one young son.

For days I was haunted by images in my mind of the desperate parent's frantically digging in the grain. I wondered how they would survive this unimaginable loss. Will this young brother ever be okay? Will they all simply drown in their sorrow? I do not know the answer. I do not even know the family. But I do know that they have consumed my thoughts for days.

In my world, I speak with people every day about loss. Surprisingly, many times my clients do not even recognize a loss when it occurs. They are often confused by their intense sadness when they sell their first home even though the plan is to move into a bigger much more fabulous spot. In their minds, they should be ecstatic to move on, but yet they are oddly sad and often brought to tears when they sign the paperwork. In matrimonial situations clients are often embarrassed by their inability to cope, particularly when they themselves had been the one to initiate the divorce. My business clients are many times startled by their anger and disappointment when an employee decides to leave. Almost never, however, do these clients describe the experience as loss.

Of course, these are but a few examples of loss and each are worthy of all the care and patience that grieving demands. In experiencing loss, however, what is most determinative is what people do with the loss after it has occurred. Once the initial shock has ended and you are through the crisis, how will you decide to let the loss impact your life? In my experience, the choice you make in defining the loss will play a key role in determining your future.

I remember a situation as a social worker that taught me volumes about defining loss. It was a Friday morning on a cold winter day and I was scheduled to be the intake worker at my busy child welfare office. This meant that I was to handle any new matter that came in the door. A challenging day was clearly in store as I was greeted with twenty fresh messages on my peg when I arrived.

I grabbed my coffee and headed straight to my office to get started; already prioritizing the stack of messages in my hand. However, when I arrived at my door I was abruptly interrupted by the receptionist. "There is a family here to see you. Please come to the front office right away." Sigh. That was all the information I was provided. I had no idea what was in store for me as I turned around and walked back down the hall to the client area.

I entered the small meeting room. Standing by the table was a man and woman, whom I presumed were the parents. They appeared agitated and anxious, but also annoyed by what I could only assume to be their short wait to see me. Behind them and off to the side seated at the table was a boy of about twelve years old, holding a small duffle bag. He was silent and void of all emotion.

I motioned to the parents to join us at the table and they promptly declined. "We won't be here long" they stated in a very matter-of-fact way. I felt unnerved by the flatness of their tone.

The father explained to me that this was their adopted son Michael. He and his wife had originally been his foster parents and then later made the decision to adopt him. Michael had been a part of their family for about six years, he stated without sentiment. The father then boldly declared that they were in my office because they had changed their mind. They no longer wanted Michael. They had come to my office on this Friday morning to return him. The mother simply nodded her head in agreement as the young boy lowered his eyes to the floor.

It was like a bomb dropped. "What? This isn't Wal-Mart!" I screamed in my head, acutely aware that this young boy was sitting right in front of me. Return him to what? This poor innocent child. And the duffle bag. Honestly, this little bag held everything he owned? I took a deep breath and calmly asked them to explain to me what was happening in the home.

The parents described some difficult behaviours (which to me were fairly typical of the pre-teen years). They then detailed their exhaustion and frustration and finally they concluded their comments declaring their unequivocal intention to walk out the door. Quite frankly, it was like they were speaking a foreign language. I couldn't make any sense of their assessment and the whole event was beyond anything my mind could comprehend. It was simply unconscionable.

The boy sat silently as I offered a range of different supports to try and get this family on track. I felt like a desperate car salesman trying to find a fit for this family; throwing out options and extras in an attempt to lure them into a conversation. To no avail. The parents, after listening to my pleas for only a short time, declined the plethora of offers, turned and walked out the door.

There I sat with this 12 year old boy and his duffle bag. A huge serving of cold, hard loss on a platter. Sadness and desperation filled the room.

The moments forward were a blur as I kicked into high gear. I was deeply concerned, obviously, that Michael would go into shock having experienced what clearly was a crisis of epic proportions. Even though I didn't have children of my own at that time, some kind of mama bear instinct took over. I wanted to right this wrong for Michael. Like the parents desperately digging in the grain, I wasn't going to let this boy suffocate in this loss.

What I was to learn later was what really shocked me.

Tragically, this wasn't Michael's first experience with loss. His father had left his mother shortly after his birth: loss number one. Then, as a toddler he was apprehended by social services since his mother was mentally ill and unable to care for him. Loss number two. Next, he was placed with his elderly grandparents, who after a few years returned him to care as at their age and stage they were unable to look after a young child. Loss three. He then bounced through foster homes until he ended up with these people who just abandoned him in my office. Loss four, five, six... Gigantic life changing losses that I assumed had done irreparable damage to this young boy.

It may seem odd, but this is where the lesson begins. Michael was resilient and accepting. Although he had obvious concern for his immediate survival, he almost instantly trusted that I would take care of him. He believed that people were inherently good and in his wise little 12 year old brain, he recognized that he had survived loss before and undoubtedly, would again. He consciously decided to be ok.

I did what any smart social worker would do to build a relationship with a 12 year old boy: I fed him. After many burgers, pizzas and other high carb meals, he opened up to me and allowed me to help him move forward. We had him placed in one of our best foster homes, we found him excellent counselling (which incidentally was discontinued early on as the psychologist felt he was quite well adjusted despite the events of his life) and we built a community around him.

I worked hard for Michael as his story and his character demanded the best of me. Ultimately, I was successful in opening his adoption file and located his birth mother; a moment I will forever treasure as a highlight of my career. With her consent and a high degree of support, they were reunited the following Christmas and Michael was able to re-establish contact with his birth family. He was gracious and grateful. He was hopeful. Most importantly, despite the many unimaginable compounded losses, Michael had decided to be happy.

We aren't all as wise as Michael. Sometimes, we have to be taught how to deal with loss. It isn't a class typically taught at school and although it is my belief that everyone should be assigned a social worker at birth, most people have little or no contact with mental health professionals during their lifetime. Dealing gracefully with loss is an art and those who are able to come out the other end stronger and well-adjusted will often add a level of quality to their life experience that is beyond measure.

I think in particular of two instances, one a favorite matrimonial client and the second, my mom.

Sarah, my matrimonial client, walked through my door a meek and quiet mouse, clearly scared to take steps on her own but fiercely determined to somehow figure it out. She had two beautiful daughters, one finishing high school and the other well on her way to achieving the career of her dreams at university. Both bright, well-adjusted kids who had likely accepted that the marriage was over long before Mom. In fact, the announcement her husband was leaving came as quite a surprise.

My client was studious and exacting. She would attend each appointment with a notebook in hand taking copious notes, role playing conversations and working to understand the dynamics of her property division. A smart, educated woman, but married to a tricky businessman whom she knew would try in every way to get the edge. She had to be brave and deliberate.

And she was. Over the course of the year we worked together to resolve the very sizeable settlement and with each successful negotiation she continued to gain momentum. She took my advice, not only on legal matters, but on strategies to cope with the loss. She was my star pupil and the results were demonstrative. She achieved a better settlement than she ever envisioned, but more remarkably, she accepted the loss of the relationship and moved into a new life with confidence and excitement. Although hurt and anger are emotions that don't disappear overnight, she developed tools to ensure these emotions wouldn't consume her. Her story is one that I share regularly as new clients enter the room with the same look of fear. The ending can be much different, if you set your mind to believe and prepare to do the hard work of dealing with a loss.

So how do we learn to deal with loss? My greatest mentor was my mom. Sadly, death was her teacher as her brother died at a young age followed by her father and brother and sister. Learning through the school of hard knocks, she used her skills to help others understand how to survive the pain and embrace the days that followed. Although she was an accountant by trade, she spent many volunteer hours at the bedside of the dying offering hope and comfort in their final days.

On her 66th birthday, my mom was diagnosed with cancer. It was not a "we can start this type of treatment" kind of cancer. No, this was the "go home and get your affairs in order" kind. The doctors wouldn't tell us how much time we had, but we were astute people. We knew time was short and we were right. My Mom died five weeks following her diagnosis.

What is remarkable about my mom's end of life journey, was that she taught us how to survive the loss. Despite her diagnosis of cancer, she became the teacher; the leader; the mentor. In those short five weeks she solidified the resolve of a family and a community. She imparted wisdom and renewed and strengthened friendships. She provided people the opportunity to say goodbye; guiding every conversation with the gentleness of a new mother caressing her young child. With absolute certainty, she made us understand that our steps following her death would be critical to our future and the future of our children. She allowed us to be sad, but not so sad that we stared too deeply at our navels. She demanded that we look beyond ourselves and promised wholeheartedly to care for each other. She forgave us. She ramped it up, loving us with such intensity recognizing fully that these feelings of love would have to last the remainder of our lifetime.

With grace and freedom, she taught us all how to die.

Those who took the opportunity to be with my Mom during that journey have told me that their lives were forever changed. It was a remarkable time which I will always treasure. Lessons of acceptance and courage were abundant as she struggled with the realities of a dying body. It was dramatic and intense, but yet filled with peace and gratitude.

These are lessons that truly can be translated to all kinds of loss. These are the lessons that can redefine the experience of loss, whatever that loss may be, in a positive and abundant way. I hope that the farming family will understand these lessons. I pray that the young brother, like Michael, will choose to be ok.  We must all understand that loss is a part of living and that in discovering our definition of our loss, we can continue to choose a strong and abundant life.

## REFLECTIONS:

1. How has loss impacted your life? What lessons have you learned?

2. Has your experience propelled you to make changes? Discuss.

3. Are you afraid of loss? If so, is the fear impacting your momentum?

4. Have you had to support someone dealing with a loss? How has this process impacted your life? Were you helpful? What were the challenges? Could you identify moments of inspiration?

## 11

*Even in laughter the heart may ache, and rejoicing may end in grief.*

*Proverbs 14:13*

## THE NEW NORMAL

In the days following the death of my mom, my family was hit by a tsunami of well-wishers. "You are in our thoughts and prayers." "Time will ease the pain." "Treasure the memories." I poured through endless well intentioned greeting card moments noting the kind messages assuring us that somehow we would be okay. And although I deeply appreciated the outpouring of support, I wondered what it all meant. The cards were filled with good advice, but to be honest, my sadness didn't allow me to believe any of it. I read and reread the material looking for some answer to end my suffering. I was searching for a clue that would tell me how long it would take until I would feel better and what I had to do to make life again seem normal.

However, my world as I currently knew it and my future as I had planned it was over. I was only thirty-six years old and I still needed my mom. This was big. And despite my searching, I found no answers.

The grief was intense. It started like an ocean wave crashing over me and pulling me swiftly to the ground. I lost my breath. I had physical pain and at times, it all seemed like more than I could handle. Each time the wave hit I wondered if I would survive. But they just kept coming. Relentless and hard.

And yet life around me carried on.

My young children didn't wait for my sorrow to pass. They needed to be fed and loved. They wanted to play. They were aged two and four; prime time for busy and fun. They didn't understand the grief nor did I want them to. Life for my girls would not stop.

My dad needed help. He and mom had the kind of marriage that you read about in story books. Always together as life partners: they were recognized in the community as one entity. A dedicated and remarkable marriage. And now my dad had lost his best friend and confident. His business partner. The love of his life. His world. He was suffering intensely and I wanted to do all I could to ease his pain.

And my work kept rolling in. Each day I had to put on a brave face to lead my staff and attend to my clients. So many of my clients knew my mom; her accounting practice and our law firm worked hand in hand. The clients were sad and afraid. They lost a trusted advisor and friend. They came to offer condolences but also to express their grief. They cried, and I counseled and consoled.

And my grandmother, my mom's mother, at age 95 was not coping well. Her health was failing at a frantic pace following my delivery of the news of Mom's cancer. From that day on, she lost her will to live. In fact, in the moment of telling her the news, I watched life slip out of her body. She could no longer survive in her apartment alone. It was time to find Grandma a new home with ongoing support and care. As I scrambled with arrangements, it was clear to me that Grandma was now dying of a broken heart. I knew of no cure.

So despite my desperate need for time to reflect, life didn't stop. In fact, in some ways it felt like the pace was quickening and I was falling behind. In some ways, it reminded me of that childhood moment when my older brother would be ahead of me on a bike ride and I, just learning and unable to keep the pace, would stop and cry. He would yell at me from the next block to just keep coming. "Don't stop and for goodness sake, quit crying like a baby" he would holler. This grief experience was similar in so many ways. I was afraid and didn't want to be left behind, alone. I had the skills to ride the bike, even though new and imperfect, but for whatever reason I just wanted to stop and cry my eyes out. I wanted to make him come back for me. Make him take care of me. But he wouldn't. My brother was pushing me to be independent and to handle that bike on my own. I needed to press on.

The grief was unpredictable. It would catch me by surprise and knock me down again, as if to remind me never to forget. The grief had control and if at any moment I thought I was in charge, I was quickly corrected. It took a long time before the familiar grocery store was a safe place. Certain aromas would bring instant tears. And months would pass before it stopped feeling like every song on the radio had some deeper meaning directed right at me. I was sad. More sad than I have ever been. And I wondered constantly when it would end.

But in time, it did get better. The sea of sadness settled and although there continued to be waves, they became smaller, and sometimes the water was calm. Eventually, I went back to that grocery store. The sweet smell of Mom's perfume or her favorite dish didn't send me into a panic. In time, I turned the radio back on and enjoyed listening, even to songs that brought back cherished memories. But it took time. More time than I wanted to spend moving through the grief and feeling all of those strong emotions that rocked my world.

Somewhere in the midst of it all, I put my sadness to work. I threw myself into advocating for improved palliative care. I recognized that not all families would have the ability to handle the dying process as we did and so the system needed to change to provide better support. It was my gift to my mom; to honour a woman who gave me life and who also taught me how to die. I used my grief to change the world in the only way I knew how. It may have saved me.

Now approaching the ten year anniversary of my mom's passing, I recognize the many quiet gifts of grief. These gifts were totally unidentifiable when I was in the midst of my pain but recognizing them now, I am in many ways a grateful recipient. Experiencing this grief has changed my outlook.

The loss of my mom will perhaps represent one of the most poignant moments in my life. And prior to the actual event, it was a moment I worried about with fearful anticipation. But now it has happened and I have survived. This is what I have learned, so far:

1.     Death is permanent. When they are gone, they are really gone. You can't pick up the phone. You can't mention something later. You can't touch them, hug them, hold them. It is over. Really over. Seems like such a simple concept but yet I can honestly say that I never understood the permanence of death until it happened.

2.     I am capable. There was a vacancy as matriarch, a role I would now have to fill. My mom handled that role perfectly and all those tasks would now fall to me as the only daughter. There were traditions to maintain, womanly advice to pass

on, history to remember, and care giving to attend to. Some of this I have learned, either by remembering her lessons or by gaining insight of my own. Other parts, I have accepted were her gifts to be honored and treasured as a memory: her legacy. I can say, however, that I now walk through each day stronger and more confident knowing that whatever falls before me, I can figure it out. Why? Because I faced what I believe to be one of the hardest lessons of my life. I have lost my mom.

3.      The bad stuff fades away. You forget the harsh words, the rough memories. By grace we are allowed after loss to wear rose coloured glasses. And we should. What good can come from reliving the negative? Embrace the positive and tell those stories. The bad was hard enough at the time that it occurred. Enough suffering.

4.      Relationships matter. People matter. Stuff doesn't matter. Again, so simple. But I swear life looks different after profound loss. There are endless songs, poems, books, quotes etc. written about this. They are right. Believe it. Say what you need to say, fix what you need to fix, and be who you want to be. Time is limited. Use it well.

5.      Life won't stop. People keep moving forward. They send you their thoughts and prayers and move on. Like a marathon, you may need to pause and catch your breath as people travel past. This is okay. As much as you want to race full out through the grieving process and cross the finish

line to normal life, you can't. Find time to reflect. Let the world carry on and carve out some time to grieve. You can't avoid it and you can't run through it. If you try, grief will knock you down and demand respect. So give it the time that it deserves. And know, eventually, you will feel better.

6.      Being afraid of death doesn't change the fact that you will face it. You will face the death of the people you love and ultimately, you too will die. Understanding the origin of that fear is helpful. Are you afraid to be alone?  Are there unsaid words? Unresolved issues? Are you afraid of your own death? Taking a hard look at these questions now may help you cope later. And maybe, you will make a change that will make all the difference.

The lesson of losing a parent was a hard one.  The suffering was intense and the sadness was immeasurable.  My mom was my best friend and my greatest champion. I have no doubt that she would be proud that I survived and even more, she would be proud that I put my grief to work.  The truth is, my mom would have demanded nothing less.  We all know we will die someday.  It is what we do with the loss we experience while we are still here that matters.

## REFLECTIONS:

1. What are you grieving? How are you responding to that loss? Where are you at in that process?

2. What have you learned so far?

3. Do you know people in your life that are dealing with grief? How does their grief impact your life? How can you be supportive? Are you learning from their experience?'

4. Can you put your grief to work? How?

## 12

*I am the light of the world. Whoever follows me will never walk in darkness, but will have the light of life.*

John 8:12

## THE WEIGHT OF REGRET:  STAY THE COURSE

I like to run. Mostly I like to run because I like to eat, but I also like to run because it is good for my head. Running is a great way to process ideas and be creative. It also relieves stress and helps me sleep at night. Overall, it allows me time to think and reflect. I have made some of my best decisions during a good jaunt.

A few years ago I ran a 5km race which also included eighteen surprise obstacles throughout the course. The obstacles ranged from scaling a wall to crawling through mud under barbed wire fences. It was totally out of character for me to participate in such hard core exercise but truthfully, the experience was completely invigorating.

While many moments of this race are forever etched in my memory, one obstacle stands out with particular clarity. The race was held on a motocross track and for this obstacle we had to drag a cement block first down and then back up to the top of a steep hill. The block was attached to a chain. This wasn't the first obstacle in the race and by no means would it be the last on this hot August afternoon. Approaching the line you could see the worry and yet, determination, on the faces of my competitors.

When I arrived at the obstacle I was handed my chain. I proceeded to move quickly with relative ease down that steep incline with this cement block chasing behind me. The block jerked and jumped down that hill and while it was tricky to control, downhill was achievable; maybe even fun.

But then came the difficult trek back up. Standing at the bottom of that hill and gazing up to the top of this steep incline, the task ahead seemed insurmountable. I pulled on that block with all my might; it was heavy and obstinate. The ground, slippery with dry powdery motocross dust, meant a few steps forward were often recanted by a slide back down of equal or more distance. There were people all around me, and while they were focused on their own journey, they were still competing feverously to reach the high ground. It was, after all, a race.

We had words, my block and I. I expressed all kinds of strong emotions as I pushed myself to reach the summit. I felt anger and frustration which was interspersed with moments of embarrassment. There were friends along the way to help, but ultimately this was my gig alone. It was a struggle and I can tell you quite honestly that I hated that block and everything it represented. But my block did not care. My block was unwilling and stubborn, unlike those of some of my competitors which seemed to surf the course with ease. I felt jealous.

Ultimately, I reached the top. I let go of that chain and ran on, never looking back and feeling a million times lighter. While I was sure I would never forget the block or the feelings it invoked, I let go and continued on my journey.

This experience can be translated into so many different life lessons. The process of reaching a goal and staying the course are the first to come to mind. The plan may start off easy, but you have to hang in through the hard parts too. Maybe the block represents a marriage or an important relationship; a life journey with many dips along the way, some deeper than others that require you to hang on tight, dig deep and stay focused. Sometimes your block cooperates and makes it easy, other times it does not. But if you can make it through the dip, you can carry on the journey with relative ease. Sometimes you have to leave the block behind and not look back.

We are all carrying burdens and regrets. They make us heavy. And despite the people in our lives that may support and encourage us along the way, this is our journey alone. We can either grab that chain with both hands and charge up the hill, saying our peace even if it falls on deaf ears to ultimately release the chain and carry on. Light. Free.

Unburdened. Or we can hang with our block forever; stuck on the same hill taking a few steps forward and then, often times, sliding back down. It can be a long hard road. And of course, carry too many blocks and you are totally paralyzed, incapable of moving forward. It's that simple.

When I think of forgiveness, true forgiveness, I think of that light feeling I had after I let go of that chain. No longer held back and able to move on to the next obstacle. How many times I have said to my daughters "say sorry like you *actually* mean it and you, my dear, need to accept her apology". This isn't a lesson reserved for 10 year olds. Why do I teach them this? Well because if they don't truly seek and grant forgiveness, they will (on either side of that process) remain chained to a block.

It is easy to see examples of moments that require us to forgive others. When others have wronged us, although difficult and rarely instantaneous, the words "I forgive you" can bring great relief to all. But what about the times we need to forgive ourselves? How do we make that happen?

In my social work career, I have worked with people who have done horrific things, acts that they often deeply regret but for whatever reason were unable to prevent. One of the most difficult to comprehend being the abuse of a child. And in working with an abuser, the issue of self-loathing can be a real challenge to overcome. Society shuns these people and forgiveness from the victim or society at large is usually unattainable. Often they live under a dark grey cloud for a very long time, maybe even a lifetime. But should they be allowed to forgive themselves and move forward? And if so, how do you let go of that chain?

The same idea can be seen in less dramatic examples. Times where we ourselves have wronged another (for much less egregious acts), and instead of addressing the issue head on and dealing with the difficult feelings and perhaps repercussions, we slide around on that slippery slope. We don't seek the forgiveness of others: so often pride is in the way. But we also don't forgive ourselves. We replay the event again and again in our minds, sometimes spinning the content. It sits with us and we are uncomfortable; burdened.

Other examples include times we have wronged ourselves by failing to reach some personal marker or goal; some standard we have set for ourselves. We too fall prey to the process of self-loathing, albeit on maybe a different scale. The lack of forgiveness results in an unwanted load and we begin to drag that block along.

The lesson is to be light. Attack the hill with a vengeance and say your peace. Accept responsibility and acknowledge your shortcomings. Have insight. But then let go and carry on. And keep your pace. After all, the next obstacle awaits.

## REFLECTIONS:

1.  Do you feel heavy? What burdens are you carrying that you could drop to lighten your load? What will it take to let go?

2.  Are you at peace? Are you able to forgive yourself and move forward despite your shortcomings? What does forgiving yourself look like?

3.  Do you know someone who is heavily burdened? How do you respond to them? How do you support them? What is your role in their burden?

## 13

*And the peace of God, which transcends all*
*understanding, will guard your hearts and your minds.*

*Phillippians 4:7*

## PUTTING HOPE TO WORK

My client's husband of 35 years went for his usual morning walk on a riverbank one morning and never returned. They were happily married. A shoe was found on the bridge nearby. That was all. Volunteers gathered and search parties were formed: every inch of that river and the surrounding area were checked for any signs of her beloved husband. For many days she held out hope, but eventually, she had to face the reality that he wasn't coming home. His body was never recovered in that fast moving river and sadly, my client will never know what happened on that beautiful July morning.

In the corners of her mind, she still wonders if he will someday walk through the door. As we meet to deal with sorting out his business affairs, she asks me if it is silly for her to still have hope.

Hope: to have a wish to get or do something or for something to happen or be true, especially something that seems possible or likely. That is the definition of hope.

When I was 12 years old I volunteered at a seniors centre for a Speech Pathologist. My job was to work with the stroke victims and help them regain their speech. Repetitive practice was recommended for these patients and so for 15 minutes each weekday, we would recite the alphabet together.

I remember Jim. A prominent member of our community, he retired from banking at age 65 to enjoy the life he had worked so hard to create. Now, at age 68, he suffered a severe stroke and lost all ability to speak. Prior to this he was an active and capable retiree. The family was understandably anxious to sign him up for this program, hoping that with a daily routine he could regain some, if not all, of his capacity to speak.

At first, Jim was happy to see me and it was obvious that determination and diligence were front and centre in his mind. Of course, as with most stroke victims, he had involuntary tears but those tears, if anything, represented excitement and happiness. Jim was prepared to tackle the task at hand and would diligently watch my face as I shaped my mouth for the sound of the letter. He would desperately try to mimic the image before him and then gradually add the sound.

Sadly, there was almost no success. While Jim's brain said one thing, his body clearly disobeyed. It was terribly frustrating for the both of us and our short sessions together soon seemed painfully long and disappointing. Nonetheless, I was committed and determined to do all I could to help "Grandpa Jim".

After only a few weeks of spending time together, Jim became increasingly agitated and frustrated. His involuntary tears didn't seem so involuntary anymore as they quickly changed to tears of sadness and frustration. I could tell he was embarrassed to be struggling to say the alphabet with a 12 year old girl. Ultimately, the very sight of me began to make him angry and so despite my honest efforts, all hope was lost. The family requested I stop coming. Jim never spoke again and I was forbidden to see him.  I was never given a chance to say good-bye.

As a 12 year old girl it was difficult to understand the complex emotions that surrounded this situation. I was sad and defeated. I had hope that my work would have resulted in magical success and I had no idea that this was highly improbable. No one bothered to explain to me the severity of his stroke and the minuet likelihood of speech recovery. My hope was clearly misplaced and not fully understanding the situation, my internal response was to record the event as a failure. My perception of hope was forever changed.

Interestingly, somewhere in the rush to help this man I had embodied the very vision of hope that both the family and the team of professionals serving Jim were holding strong. Undoubtedly a young, smart girl would inspire Jim to speak again! It was like they were scripting a Hollywood film. But when the hope was lost, my role was instantly cut. It was like the very thought of having hope was frivolous and they all wanted to erase any trace of evidence that might reveal that they even considered hope an option. This too, deeply impacted me.

As a child, we are taught to have hope. They tell us to dream the impossible, hope for great things and believe the unbelievable. However when you magically hit number 18, everything changes. No more Santa, Easter Bunny or hope. Somehow the act of holding out hope becomes clouded in shame. It is seen as a weakness or a reflection of insecurity. It is something you should only express with caution, and even then quietly and in a reserved manner. Strong people accept the facts and move on and any inability to do so may reflect other, more deeply rooted problems. If we are to have hope, we require the permission and acceptance of others. Hope is seen as rash and extreme behaviour. Bizarre.

From seemingly insignificant events - "I hope my house deal closes on time" to life altering moments "I hope my missing child returns home" - the act of saying these wishes out loud attracts a negative undertone. Are we really so afraid that believing that the extraordinary is worth hoping for that we refuse to allow ourselves those moments of solace? I have often wondered if people fear that hoping for something better will bring upon a much worse or negative event?

When I meet with clients to take instructions on their wills I am often quite clear in explaining to them that actually preparing a will does not make you die. It seems strange, but clients in that moment will start to believe if they write it, it will happen. A paranoia sets in and some clients suffer great anxiety about putting pen to paper. I am quick to assure them that yes, there is clear and reliable evidence that eventually you will die. However, the act of writing your Last Will and Testament does not hasten death. We know that saying, thinking or believing something, even events that are abundantly possible, doesn't necessarily make the event happen. If we had that kind of power, I would suggest buying a lotto ticket amongst other things. Yet in that moment of considering final wishes, people trick their mind to believing it to be so.

Strangely however, in times when a hopeful mind is so desperately needed, people feel embarrassed, ashamed or insecure to even say the impossible, or even the possible, out loud. Not all people. And the people that are able to stroll past this insecurity, provide a fine example of why the solace of hope can be so remarkable.

I recall an incident in recent years when my husband and I were driving to a Christmas Party. We had shuffled our kids to their next location and scrambled out the door. We were already a touch late at 6pm, as we headed on the dark winter highway to our destination.

As we were close to our approach we could see vehicles in the distance pulling off onto the shoulder of the highway. Strangely, we next saw a lady running towards us frantically waiving her arms. Distracted and confused by all the activity, my husband swerved at the last moment to avoid the human body laying in the middle of the highway. We instantly pulled over to assist and do all we could to help the people around us.

The next morning upon attending at my office, there was an urgent telephone message. My client was calling requesting a meeting as her brother had been killed in a pedestrian accident on the highway the night prior. I was stunned. First, struck by grief realizing who was lying before me just a few hours prior and second, I wasn't sure how the family would react knowing that I was first on the scene after the accident occurred.

One should never underestimate or assume. This was an unbelievable family filled with profound hope and grace in a very proud and robust way. After hearing my story, they embraced me with compassion and care. They were deeply concerned that I had witnessed this horrific event and the impact that this would have on my future. I, for my part, was extending condolences to them for the loss of their dear beloved brother. They wanted to do something for me to show me their gratitude for being present. I knew exactly the answer to help us all through this devastating situation.

The driver of the vehicle who had innocently struck their brother was in his mid-twenties. He was on his way to the department store to pick up Christmas decorations. His three year old son was in the back seat of the truck at the time of the accident and I remember vividly talking to him about his cowboy boots to distract him from the chaos. Both were physically unharmed, but the man was suffering extreme emotional turmoil that night as my husband and I paced the edge of the highway with him until the emergency personnel arrived. I had never met this man before, but I had no doubt this experience would haunt him forever.

My request to the family was simple. I asked them to meet this young man. I asked them to let him share his sadness and his need for forgiveness. I wanted them to provide him some form of closure.

The family instantly agreed. Not only did they meet and forgive him, they welcomed him with open and loving arms to the funeral of their brother. They listened to his expressions of utter sadness and remorse and they comforted and consoled. They helped him recognize that this was an innocent accident; the evidence of which was totally clear. They told him that their lives would now forever be connected and that they accepted him.

They then closed the discussion by asking him to be hopeful for the future, both for himself and his young son. It was a remarkable moment. They were deeply worried about the impact this event would have on such a young man and it troubled them to think it may stop or even slow him in his tracks. In their minds, their brother had lived a long and full life and he wouldn't want it any other way. And so, in order to honour the memory of their brother they demanded that this young man have hope for the future. The family said that these words, even at this early time, physically lifted the pain off of this young man. There was closure.

Find hope in your life and embrace it. Share it with the world. Permit yourself and others to live the extraordinary lives you deserve. We have but one chance, take all that is good and amplify it. Let hope be your guide to all future interactions and attend to them with abundance and faith. This is the gift we have been given.

## REFLECTIONS:

1.  Do give yourself permission to be hopeful? What do you hope for? Do you share your hope with others?

2.  What is the source of your hope? Is the desired outcome achievable? How can you work towards success?

3.  What are the hopes of the people in your life? Are they rational? Achievable? How do you respond when their hopes are expressed to you?

---

## 14

*There is a time for everything, a season for every activity under the heavens: a time to be born and a time to die, a time to plant and a time to uproot, a time to kill and a time to heal, a time to tear down and a time to build.*

*Ecclesiastes 3*

## ENJOY THE BLOOM

Imagine, a young couple strolling on a beach at sunset with the gentle waves lapping against their bare feet. A mother, softly caressing the forehead of her newborn child as she sleeps peacefully in her arms. Two friends, enjoying a good laugh at an outdoor cafe on a bright summer's day. An elderly couple, simply holding hands. These are all images that help us feel peaceful, calm and content. They warm and soothe us like fresh homemade pie served straight out of the oven. We all yearn for moments like these. We seek moments that will make us feel free, alive and protected. Moments that will satisfy our soul and embrace all of our inner needs. We need moments that make the clock stop and take our breath away.

We all desire moments of true love.

The need to be loved is at the very core of our being.

And in working in the field of helping people, every file that I touch is somehow connected to that base emotion of love. Good or bad, right or wrong, that need to be loved and accepted infiltrates every aspect of our lives. We must not resist, but rather embrace the need and find those moments to create fulfillment.

I used to spend many hours working alongside my mom in her greenhouse. I remember taking great care to ensure the trays had proper drainage, preparing the soil and then wrapping the trays to warm. Then we would delicately place those tiny seeds ever so gently in the soil covering them perfectly and then carefully adding water and nutrients. Each day we would wait and watch with great anticipation, checking for signs of life. We were hoping our love would be returned.

There would be cheers of great excitement when the first seedlings arrived. We would attend to them with tender care giving them everything we could to ensure a healthy start. Eventually, we would repot them and then, when we believed they were ready, we would move them to the big world outside.

Once outside, we would continue to care for them, but it was different. Sometimes we forgot, or got too busy. Beautiful summer days had many distractions that would draw us away. Those forgotten plants didn't fare so well. And if we left them too long without the needed attention, it was sometimes impossible to bring them back. They were never quite the same. Some years Mother Nature took over, and despite our best intentions, survival was beyond our control. But sometimes, with dedication and a little luck, we could nurse them back to health.

But the plants we gave regular attention to, the ones we loved unconditionally and made sure we provided for, those plants would usually flourish and grow. They would produce beautiful flowers as a sign of their reciprocating love and we would treasure their beauty and proudly show them off to friends. We would enjoy them for all that they were.

And eventually, like all good things, the snow would fly and it would all come to an end.

Like a delicate plant, most of us know what we need to do to foster and grow love, but sometimes we fail. If initially we don't prepare the ground properly, it is unlikely our love will flourish. If later, we get distracted and forget to focus on the important task at hand, our love will not survive. And sometimes we recognize our shortcomings and in desperation we try to get it all back. Sometimes we are successful. Other times the relationship is beyond repair. The damage has gone too far and cannot be reversed.

Sometimes there are elements out of our control. Outside influences infiltrate that are bigger and more powerful and there is nothing we can do to stop them. We have to ride out the storm, doing our best to control the damage. After it is over, we have to assess the situation and then try to piece it back together.

And sometimes, it just simply isn't meant to be. Whatever the cause or reason, our love will not flourish. And we have to let go.

But if it does work, we must cherish the beauty of it all and be proud of this great accomplishment. We must continuously nourish our love and ensure that it has all things necessary for survival. We must attend. And we must always recognize that, like the flower, someday love will come to an end regardless of its strength. And in that moment, what you have lost will matter. So enjoy love while it blooms for all that it offers.

A twenty six year old man came into my office, confused and troubled. The woman he married had changed substantially in their short three years of marriage. They started out (he believed) deeply in love, they had a child, and are now expecting a second. He was raised in a traditional family that demonstrated at all levels what is good about marriage, and as a result he had no concept of divorce or separation. She, however, came from a broken family and had suffered loss and trauma at a young age, which I suspected, she had never properly grieved.

She was now threatening divorce. She was

producing emotional, erratic behaviour, all designed to push him away. Like a toddler, she was having tantrums to test the limits of their marriage. He, for his part, loved her deeply and was desperate to understand her irrational behaviour. It would seem, however, that she felt unlovable.

As we unraveled her history together, he came to appreciate her fear of rejection. We acknowledged her history and the likely impact on her soul. He showed levels of compassion that I truly did not expect. And remarkably, he reacted in a way that gave me great hope.

Instead of flight, he chose to fight for the marriage. He declared that he would love her more. He would love her through this. This twenty six year old husband would prove to his wife that she was lovable. He was determined to nurture this plant for the sake of the marriage and the children. Having a new understanding of the behaviour, he was invigorated. He acknowledged the challenge ahead and together, we engaged a counselor. His reaction was both surprising and delightful to me, a file I was pleased to close. Hopefully forever.

To love unconditionally is hard. There are moments in any relationship where love is not the first emotion to rise to the surface. But we can all agree that a response predicated on love normally produces the best results. So how do we achieve this?

The key is understanding a very basic concept: we are only in control of ourselves. We cannot control what others think, how they behave or how they choose to react. If we truly understand this, then we can be free to focus on love because from this foundational soil relationships can flourish.

It means that we must first prepare ourselves. We must love and accept ourselves for all that we are and all that we may someday be. We must embrace our beauty, inside and out, and challenge ourselves to make good choices always. Despite all of the things that have happened in our lives and all of the storms we have endured, we must be determined to be well and we must try to do all things to ensure that we are.

From this foundation, we can build positive loving relationships.

We must step out of our own needs and wants and attend to others. Be selfless. We should endeavor to fulfill meaning and purpose through acts of kindness and goodness. To use patience, tolerance and understanding to bring out the best in others thereby acknowledging and accepting the very best in ourselves.

We must pause and see our role and responsibility in events and transactions and acknowledge our wrongdoings. We must endeavor to always make good choices for ourselves and those around us. The answers won't always be easy, but coming from a correct foundation they will be acceptable.

We must accept love freely and voluntarily with no ulterior motive or attachment. Just simply to feel worthy of joy and goodness. And we must believe that we, like others, deserve positive results.

We must work through change and dysfunction in a spirit of cooperation and resolution. We must be willing to alter plans and accommodate. We must not be stubborn or indignant.

We should allow ourselves to feel challenged and alive; competitive but not vengeful. We must strive to bring joy to others. To share freely. We must be open to new experiences and ideas. We must push ourselves to be fulfilled in all ways and we must accept that this picture is different for everyone.

Nurture yourself and love will grow. Embrace the love and it will survive. Prepare for the storms, for they will come. But know that sometimes different is okay. And always recognize that loss is inevitable, no matter your strength. Love deeply, passionately and with full commitment. And enjoy the bloom.

## REFLECTIONS:

1. What is your image of true love?

2. Are you loveable?  Why or why not.

3. How do you demonstrate love to those around you? How do you need to be loved?

4. What have you done to show love recently?

## 15

*Taste and see the Goodness of the Lord.*

*Psalm 34:8*

## PUTTING THE PIECES (BACK) TOGETHER

In the end, it is about choices. How you choose to respond to a connection, an opportunity or a loss will matter. Whether you choose to engage will make a difference. Will you choose to love and be loved?

From the moment you wake up in the morning until you lay your head down at night you will be faced with choices. So choose well. Always. And recognize that there are, in fact, choices. You do have control but you also have responsibility. Maybe you will choose to sit on the floor and listen. Maybe you will choose a pause. Maybe, like Michael in Chapter 10, you will choose to be okay.

We know that we cannot control the choices of others, as frustrating as that may be. But yet we fixate on their reactions and responses. We wonder about their opinions and we seek their acceptance. Redirecting that energy to live with passion and focus on balanced and confident choices will grant us freedom. It will hand us the reigns and allow us to love freely and accept recognition. It will permit us to be present in our life and confident in our choices.

As parents, we hope our children will choose well. From picking snacks to avoiding drugs, childhood is full of choices. Why is it then, as adults, we stop seeing choices for ourselves. We often find ourselves stuck in a rut of unhappiness or lacking personal fulfillment. Something changes when we enter adulthood. Life, loss and fear impact our abilities to choose well. Sadly, many of us stop dreaming.

What have we learned? Change your sheets. Put yourself out there and connect with interest. Serve. Serve. Serve. Be all in for your own life and take time to enjoy the bloom. Each day, set the stage to be Molly at age 87 and maintain that healthy perspective. Try to remind yourself regularly that your life need not be a whisper. Be more than present, be a presence in your life and the lives of others. And acknowledge that ultimately, you too can choose to die with grace.

The good news is that it is all there for the taking. The choice is yours. How will your next chapter unfold? Your choices will matter so resolve today to pick carefully. Within everyone's ordinary, exists the extraordinary. Take time to acknowledge your extraordinary and decide today to live a life with everyday grace.

## REFLECTIONS:

1. Do you recognize the extraordinary you in your ordinary life? What part of you makes you the most proud?

2. What steps can you take to empower the best version of you?

3. Do you acknowledge the extraordinary in others? How do you show recognition?

4. What does your tomorrow look like? How will you choose your everyday grace?

## ACKNOWLEDGEMENTS:

The experience of writing this book has been extremely fulfilling and enriching. I am grateful to my many clients and friends who have influenced my days and graced my life by sharing their stories. Clearly, this book would not have been possible without them.

Thank you to Gail Jansen-Kesslar for your kind and gentle wisdom. And to Shane Haughian for your vision. You are both treasures who so quickly understood what I was trying to accomplish.

I am grateful to my friend and mentor, Christopher Flett. Chris you are a champion beyond words. You have challenged me to deliver my best self and to always believe that anything is possible. Thank you.

To my Dad who stands with me each day and guides me on my journey, I love you for all of that and so much more. Thank you for believing in this book and always believing in me.

To my daughters, Emma and Sophie, who make my life full and amazing, thank you for all that you are and all that you do. I hope that you will continue to dream and also see that anything is possible. And know that I will always be by your side.

And to my husband Chad, there are no words for all that you do in my life. You are my everyday grace.

## ABOUT THE AUTHOR:

Carla was born and raised in small town Saskatchewan; her mother a practicing accountant and her father a practicing lawyer. Carla was immersed early in the practical aspects of ordinary living involving financial and legal issues.

Carla first obtained her Social Work Degree (BSW) and practiced as a social worker often dealing with abused children in disadvantaged families. In this capacity, Carla developed an appreciation and respect for the desperate lives of the underprivileged members of our society.

As a social worker, Carla found herself in court on many occasions and saw great opportunity to effect change as a lawyer. She entered law school in Saskatchewan and graduated with great distinction. She continues an active law practice in small town Saskatchewan in partnership with her father.

Carla was greatly impacted by the sudden illness and death of her mother in 2008. This life change motivated her to become involved in advancing the principals of palliative care in her community and across the country. She has volunteered extensively in this field and was recognized for her work by the Queen Elizabeth II Diamond Jubilee Medal.

Besides a busy law practice, Carla is married and loves spending time with her two beautiful daughters, Emma and Sophie.

61091771R00081

Made in the USA
Charleston, SC
15 September 2016